Pellew Street Horror
& other Strange True tales

Tom Slemen

Copyright © 2013 Tom Slemen

All rights reserved.

ISBN-10: 1489503080
ISBN-13: **978-1489503084**

DEDICATION

For my great friend, John Magin Kennedy

CONTENTS

The Club	1
The Alibi	4
Hellbound for Halloween	8
Judge Bracey	12
The Ghost of David Eccles	17
When the Devil Goes to Church	22
My Ragged Valentine	25
The Pellew Street Horror	30
A Message from Mr Smith	35
Thingybob	39
Some Haunted Liverpool Shops	44
Skeleton Crew	48
Headlines in Advance	53
Hotel in Another Dimension	58
The Naked Lady of Islington	63
Take it Easy	68

Monsieur Meganique	74
Warnings from the Future	77
Snakes Alive	81
Voice Across the Mersey	84
Lunar Telepathy	88
Lonely Hearts	92
A West Derby Haunting	94
Coming to a Screen Near You	97
No Place Like a Haunted Home	100
The Odd Couple	104
Head Case	108
Behind the Green Door	113
Mr Stranks	118
The Visitor	121
The Takers	126

ACKNOWLEDGMENTS

The author would like to thank the staff at the Liverpool Records Office, and also the staff at Sydney Jones Library for the use of their microfilm machines.

THE CLUB

On the Friday night of 5 January 1968, a West Derby man in his early twenties named Martin Whyte was driven to Birkenhead via the Queensway Tunnel by his Uncle Ron, who lived in Tranmere. Ron had spent Christmas and New Year at his sister's house in Liverpool, and was now returning home. He dropped his nephew off near Conway Street around 7.30pm and drove home. Martin met up with a friend named David at Hamilton Square, and the two young men went in search of a good club. What they found instead was quite bizarre. In a turning off Cleveland Street the lads came to an archway, where psychedelic music was heard. Two smiling girls, aged about 17 or 18, stood by a door, and they beckoned Martin and David. The lads stepped forward, and the girls put silken black blindfolds on them and guided them into the 'club'. At the end of a very long passage the blindfolds were removed, and under a vast arched ceiling, there was an enormous space, possibly the interior of an old warehouse. Around three hundred men and women danced and writhed, and many were naked. A dim red ceiling lamp illuminated this Pompeian scene, and the walls, which glistened with perspiration, were adorned with pentagrams and drawings (in chalk and paint) of goat-headed figures. Through the heady atmosphere of aromatic vapour mingling with cigarette smoke and alcoholic odour, a middle-aged woman of striking beauty with unusually dark eyes and long red hair danced up to Martin and set about seducing him. David was similarly beguiled by a thin teenaged girl in black with hypnotic green eyes. With a solemn look on her elfin face, she shouted, 'I will liberate you,' – but her words were barely audible over the musical din. David smiled and danced the night away with the girl, whose name, she seriously maintained, was Immaculata. Martin, a virgin who had never had a girlfriend, was a nervous wreck, and he felt very uncomfortable by the attention he was receiving from his mature admirer. He learned her name was Lucinda. She plied him with a fiery ruby drink that tasted like sweet rum until his mind whirled. All through that night, Martin kept asking where David had gone, but Lucinda would stroke his hair and caress him. The atmosphere was hot and oppressive, and several times Martin made a break from Lucinda and looked for a way out the club, but there wasn't a doorway to be found. He walked the perimeter of the wall and found a narrow opening that led to a stinking room used by both sexes as a toilet, but he couldn't find a way out of the accursed club. He asked several people how to get out and they never answered. What felt like tortured hours of time passed by, and a silhouette appeared on a stage where musicians had been performing. It was a man with horns! Through the blue haze of tobacco and marijuana smoke, Martin squinted with stinging eyes at the surreal figure on stage. The horns were really attached to his forehead, and could not possibly be stuck on like some Halloween accessories. Martin went cold. Everyone cheered, and the devil-like stranger spoke in an echoing yet gelid voice. Martin closed his eyes, made the sign of the cross, and prayed for God to deliver him from this satanic club. When he opened his eyes he saw the long passage he'd walked down earlier when he was blindfolded, and he rushed through it, out into the cool night air. He wandered the freezing night streets of Birkenhead, too afraid to return to Cleveland Street, to that archway. He walked to his Uncle Ron's home in Tranmere and told him what had happened, but Ron assumed his nephew had simply visited some Bohemian club. Martin slept at his uncle's home, but all throughout the night he suffered recurrent lucid nightmares of Lucinda swooping down on him from the ceiling.

On the following day in the afternoon, a fog enveloped the region, and Martin boarded a ferry home to Liverpool. As the ferry left the landing stage, Martin thought he heard a woman's voice call his name. He looked around and saw only a handful of people on deck, and the voice obviously hadn't been uttered by any of them. Then Martin casually gazed into the grey icy waters of the January Mersey, and his heart jumped into his mouth. A woman's face was moving through the waves, following the ferry. He pointed the eerie spectacle out to an elderly passenger, and he gasped and said someone must have fallen overboard. Martin leaned over the safety rail and stared in horror. It was Lucinda. Her long red hair trailed in the icy waters behind her. No normal person, no human could swim in the River at that speed in such cold temperatures. Others saw that face, and Martin told them who she was but the ferry passengers couldn't comprehend his claims. Martin ran to the front of the ferry in terror, expecting her to come on deck. Once again he said a prayer with his eyes clenched, and as soon as the ferry docked at Liverpool he ran off, homewards into the fog. He kept glancing back as he ran up the landing stage bridge, which was angled at a steep incline at that time because the tide was out. Martin reached the bus terminal at the Pier Head, out of breath and shaking, trying to make sense of the what he had seen. After a wait of fifteen minutes, his bus arrived, and he was only too glad to get away from the waterfront. At his home on Leyfield Road, Martin sat in front of the open fire in the parlour with his hands cupped around a mug of tea. He told his mother what had happened, and she wondered if someone had drugged her son's drink and made him hallucinate the things he described. Martin told his mum he was concerned about David, and had a feeling something had happened to him in that club, and Mrs Whyte said she'd use her next-door neighbour's telephone to phone David's house and see if everything was okay. Around 5.15pm Mrs Whyte went next door and her neighbour kindly allowed her to use the phone to call David's mother. It turned out that David was fine, and had come home drunk and covered with lipstick kisses around four in the morning. Martin eventually calmed down when he learned his friend was alright, and by 6pm he was watching his favourite show on the telly - *The Monkees*, featuring America's answer to the Beatles.

Martin went to bed around midnight, and sat up listening to his old Dansette radio. He dozed off to the whispers of Radio Luxembourg as the medium-wave station drifted slowly back and forth on the tides of the ether. At one point in the wee small hours, Martin groggily opened one eye, reached out to switch off the bedside lamp, and then attempted to turn off the radio, but clumsily nudged the tuning dial to a dead band of faint white noise that was punctuated with random clicks and static.

At some unknown hour of that morning, Martin felt something leaning on him in his bed. He opened his eyes with a start and found he couldn't move an inch. He was paralysed. Something was pressing down on his chest. The room was dark and the ceiling – which was all that he could see – was a very dim shade of grey. The radio was crackling loud. A face swam into view. It was Lucinda's face. She grinned and her dark eyes were now huge black holes, devoid of irises. Her mouth opened and formed a black disc in the wan light of the room. It grew impossibly wide, and this terrified the paralysed young man more than anything. He thought she was trying to bite into his face. He squeezed his eyes shut and tried to shout, but his mouth wouldn't open. Somewhere, from the depth of his soul perhaps, he somehow managed to summon up the power of volition, and suddenly screamed out. He opened his eyes, and finding the woman's face was still there, he tried to punch it, but his arms responded sluggishly. He spat in her face and then pushed her away. As he slid sideways out the bed, he fell to his knees, feeling so weak and drained, and he heard his mother shouting something out next door in her room. Martin managed a second, but feeble scream, and there were footfalls on the landing outside his bedroom. The pale face of Lucinda seemed so sad and disappointed-looking, as if she couldn't understand why Martin had rejected her. Her shadowy outline became thinner than a broom handle, and she vanished in an instant. The door burst open, and Martin's mother and father hurried in. The light was switched on and Mr Whyte picked his son up and sat him on the bed. When Martin told his parents what had happened, they naturally believed he had suffered nothing more than a nightmare, and advised him to go back to sleep. Martin's nerves were too frayed by the spinechilling visitation, and he sat up in bed with the light on, listening to the radio all night in a very edgy state. On the following Sunday morning, he decided to go to morning Mass at his church, thinking it would afford him some measure of divine protection against Lucinda. This worked, and for ten years he never saw the strange woman, although he had the occasional nightmare about her. When Martin caught up with David one weekend, he asked him what had happened at that club on Cleveland Street, and his friend told him that "Immaculata" had made love to him in front of a number of people in a corner of the club, and he hadn't set eyes on her since. He had visited the club, but it seemed to have closed down. Martin asked David about the man with horns who had appeared on the stage, but his friend said he couldn't remember anything about that part of the night as he was too far gone with the drink. Martin didn't believe this, and he noticed a drastic change in David's personality. He was no longer outgoing and cheerful, but very sarcastic and quite morbid. Eventually, Martin stopped hanging round with David.

One afternoon in the autumn of 1978, Martin was in Liverpool city with his wife Sue. The couple were browsing in Blacklers on Great Charlotte Street, when Martin noticed a familiar-looking shopper staring at him in the store. It was Lucinda, and she hadn't changed a bit in the ten years that had elapsed since he had seen her. The weird woman was looking at Martin's wife with an expression of pure hatred. Martin grabbed his wife's hand, and as she asked him what the matter was, he pulled her out into the street and walked as far as Hanover Street before he told her what must have seemed like a far-fetched tale concerning the mysterious supernatural woman. Sue had never known her husband to lie to her, and she could see something had obviously scared him. Out of curiosity, Martin made two trips to Cleveland Street in an effort to find the archway which shielded the club entrance, but on both occasions he was unable to locate it. Martin related this unearthly tale to me in 2002, and I mentioned it on the Billy Butler Show on Radio Merseyside. Several people got in touch to say they'd had very similar experiences, but all of them said the unidentified club they had visited was off Dale Street, close to North John Street. Not one caller mentioned the mysterious establishment in Birkenhead. However, all of the callers to the station mentioned an archway, being blindfolded and being escorted into an underground vault with an arched ceiling, with the same type of orgies going on that Martin described. All of these reports had the incidents taking place between 1970 and 1972. As with the Cleveland Street incident, the callers to the radio station all described how they tried to find the unknown club during the daytime. What are we to make of these bizarre reports? Are they truly supernatural occurrences, or were they merely the result of too much drink and perhaps even drugs? I personally feel the truth is much more sinister, and we may learn more one day.

THE ALIBI

In December 1952, a smoke-laden, choking smog blanketed most parts of Britain. It became so dense down south that cattle at Smithfield Market were asphyxiated by it, over two thousand people with respiratory problems died, and road, rail and air transport ground to a halt. Liverpool also had a taste of the soot-laden fog for three days in a row, and those three days were marked by a very peculiar incident that no one has ever satisfactorily explained. I have had to change a few surnames and details, but I can assure you that the story that follows is true.

Vinnie Monash was an habitual thief, which was a shame, because the rest of the Monashes, who all lived off Scotland Road, were a respectable, hard-working family, honest as the day is long. By the age of twenty-one, Vinnie had developed a passionate hatred towards a certain local detective - whom we shall call Rockerby. Some would say that Detective Rockerby was also obsessed with Vinnie, whom he knew to be responsible for a spate of burglaries, but the young thief was as slippery as an eel when it came to convicting him. In the summer he had even tried to charge the young Scottie Road villain with angling without a licence (which would incur a twenty pound fine) when he caught him fishing in Sefton Park, but instead, Vinnie whipped Detective Rockerby's backside with his fishing rod and ran off amidst howls of laughter from the other young rogues.

This was now assault, but Vinnie went to ground, and no one seemed to have any idea where he was. Shortly afterwards, a number of warehouses were broken into off Vauxhall Road, and an informer told the police that Vinnie Monash was behind the break-ins. Vinnie's home on Richmond Row was stormed by Detective Rockerby and some of his colleagues, but Vinnie was not to be found. His mother and youngest sister Tina, broke down in tears, when questioned by the detective, for they missed Vinnie dreadfully and they too wondered what had become of him.

Summer slipped into autumn, and the days tumbled away like the falling leaves in the city's parks, until December was upon the Monash family, and the thought of Christmas without young Vinnie was unbearable for them. Then came the smog and it provided the twilight criminals of Liverpool with a useful carboniferous cloak to aid and abet them in their nefarious activities.

Many policemen, in the course of their careers, develop a sense of hyper-intuition - an uncanny, almost psychic hunch, which allows them to predict the behaviour of criminals. And so it was that Detective Rockerby had the strong feeling that absentee Vinnie was about to rob a certain tobacconists on Scotland Road. So convinced was he, that he abandoned all his other duties and lay in wait under an archway facing the shop in question. A young constable reluctantly stood shivering alongside his boss, dreading the thought of the long cold night that lay before them. As they blew on their fingers and stamped their feet to keep warm, the worsening smog gradually caused the city and its inhabitants to fade away into nothingness.

At 8.30pm, a policeman's whistle screamed out into the grey limbo and Rockerby caught a fleeting glimpse of Vinnie's silhouette, sprinting through the Cimmerian gloom. He and the constable bolted after him with another policeman already giving chase. Vinnie must have been unbalanced, because, despite his dire predicament, he found time to swipe the helmet clean off the head of the policeman who was standing on point duty at the corner of Ellenborough Street. "The little bastard is heading for home!" panted Rockerby, his lungs ready to explode, as they entered Chaucer Street. The younger and fitter constable accompanying him managed to keep up with Vinnie for a time, but eventually, through the treacly murk, he could see the bold burglar getting fainter, as he bolted pell-mell down Rose Hill towards Richmond Row.

Within a quarter of an hour, Detective Rockerby and five police constables were hammering on the door of Vinnie's house, ready to charge him with attempted robbery. All the curtains were drawn, and Mrs Monash answered.

"Is Vinnie in, Mrs Monash?"

The poor woman looked lost for words when Rockerby told her what had just taken place, and did not seem able to fully comprehend what he was saying. Eventually, she managed, "Yes, Vinnie's in there. Go in, go on."

"At last!" thought Rockerby. "The moment I've been waiting for, for so long." and he rushed into the parlour, itching to get the handcuffs on the young villain. However, he was pulled up short by the sight of a coffin, laid out on a funeral bier. Even when told that Vinnie had died, Rockerby refused to believe it. When Mr Monash heard this, he swore at the detective and instructed a neighbour to remove the coffin lid. And there was Vinnie Monash, laid out in his burial shroud, eyes closed peacefully - but the miscreant had an eerie grin on his face. Apparently, he had died in his sleep a few days back. Rockerby could do nothing but stammer out an apology, and head straight for the nearest pub.

Vinnie was laid to rest the next day. It was as if the lad had returned from death to taunt his old adversary, just one last time...

HELLBOUND FOR HALLOWEEN

On the night of Halloween, in 1892, without any warning whatsoever, the Devil made an appearance at a house on Ranelagh Street which belonged to tobacconist, Harold Spencer. It all started with a huge ominous shadow, which glided stealthily up a bedroom wall; an impossible shadow, which did not seem to be cast by someone in the normal way. A chamber pot was thrown at the menacing silhouette, and it vanished for about an hour, but at one o'clock in the morning the bed in the guest bedroom began to shake, and the two young people under the covers - John and Anne Walker - lodgers of the Spencers, were startled from their uneasy slumbers.

The shadow was back, this time accompanied by foul-smelling odours, in particular the aroma of burning sulphur. The screams that pierced that still October morning alerted Mr Spencer and his wife, as well as the Wrights - their next door neighbours at Number 11 Ranelagh Street. Anne Walker leapt out of the now shuddering, levitating bed, threw open the bedroom window, and screamed out of it at the top of her voice, thus attracting the attention of PC Henry Kermode. He called up to ask the hysterical young woman what the matter was, and she gave an unintelligible reply, in which he could only pick out the words 'persecution' and 'Satan'.

PC Kermode was soon joined by the colleague he was supposed to meet on his beat at Waterloo Place, by the Lyceum - PC Charlie Kefford. Both constables stood listening to the racket going on at Number 13, and knocked loudly on the door until Harold Spencer answered in his nightshirt and night-cap. He tried to reassure the officers of the law that his guests had simply been drinking and were in high spirits, but he promised that he would soon calm them down. Nevertheless, screams continued to rip through the night air and then a cloud of soot billowed out of the top windows. One by one, window blinds were parted in the grand Adelphi, as rudely awakened guests looked out to find the source of the racket.

The police could not allow such a disturbance of the peace to continue on their beat and so they stormed the house and hiked up the narrow stairs, until they arrived in the guest bedroom, just in time to witness an enormous shadow of a horned man sink into the floor. John and Anne Walker were huddled together in a corner, their face blackened with soot. Upon hearing deep maniacal laughter echoing from beneath the floorboards, the two policemen exchanged glances expressing a reluctance to get involved and they promptly left, after issuing the couple with a severe warning not to disrupt the peace of the neighbourhood in the future. The persecutions started again in earnest one Saturday evening later that year, when John Walker came across a little ragged-clothed girl, carrying a doll on Clayton's Lane, which ran behind Ranelagh Street. He bent down and asked, "Are you lost, little girl?" but she looked up at him to reveal a sinister devilish face with a long hooked nose and black-rimmed eyes.

"No, but your soul is," replied what could only have been the Devil, disguised this time as a child. The doll's face suddenly became animated, breaking into a grin and spitting at John, who shrank back in revulsion. John Walker was rumoured to have committed some grave misdemeanour, which he later bitterly regretted, but no one knows just what this act was. He was a highly religious man, and he seems to have been the object of demonic persecution from 1892, but no one knows why.

Of course, the Devil can, and often does, choose to persecute anyone without a reason; even Popes have been possessed. There were rumours of Walker assaulting a girl and burying her in the cellar of Number 13 Ranelagh Street in September 1892. I talked to a descendant of Walker's recently. He told me that seven years after John Walker was interred in his grave, his wife also died. When the grave was reopened to lay her coffin on top of John's, a shocking discovery was made. His coffin was empty. The underside was smashed in, and a deep hole ran down from that grave to God knows where ... to Hell, perhaps?

JUDGE BRACEY

Out of all the manifest spirits that I have investigated, I find the enigmatic ones, which defy most explanations, the most fascinating - just like the ones featured in the following story.

In June 1965, a 40-year-old travelling salesman man from West Sussex named Jim Hughes booked a room at the Mycroft Hotel on Mount Pleasant. Jim's room was comfortable and clean enough, and he intended to stay at the hotel for a week. On the first night at the Mycroft, Jim awoke in his bed and found himself paralysed. One half of the room was bathed in subdued light from the street-lamp outside and the other half was as dark as the interior of a tomb. As Mr Hughes gazed up helplessly from his pillow, an ominous figure came into view – a figure in ermine robes and a judge's full-bottomed horsehair wig, and what's more, a black mask covered his entire face. 'This has got to be a dream,' Mr Hughes tried to whisper to himself, but even his tongue was unable to flex a millimetre. A pair of stark, unsound-looking eyes peeped out of two holes in the black mask, and a mean thin mouth was visible through an elliptical hole in the velvety fabric. That mouth moved: 'Mr Hughes, you have been summoned before me, Judge Bracey. The charge is desertion of your child. How do you plead?'

Waves of guilt and remorse coursed through Hughes, and in his mind he saw his little girl's sad face. He hadn't seen Penny or her mother for almost seven months. He'd been meaning to make a trip down to Littlehampton to see them but...

The weirdly-attired night-time phantasm rambled on loudly about the salesman's neglect of his wife and daughter. Hughes prayed for the ability to move, but couldn't even budge his big toe. Surely one of the hotel guest's would hear the booming voice of this eerie madman? Thought Hughes, but no one came. Pointing a finger, the masked magistrate screamed 'Guilty!' and Hughes blacked out. He found himself as a child in the year 1931, when his father walked out on him. He was clinging in vain to his father's leg as his dad opened the vestibule door for the last time. He watched him walk away down the street, bound for the railway station, and on to a new life with another family. That day, little Jimmy thought he'd die from his broken heart because it hurt so much. The salesman woke in tears, now fully able to move, with morning sunlight blazing into the room. He left the Mycroft Hotel that day, bought presents for his wife and daughter, and caught the train down south to see them. He assumed "Judge Bracey" was merely a figment of his conscience, but little did he know that a black-masked adjudicator had haunted several other people in Liverpool, but although the other manifestations of ghostly judges did not identify themselves, it's highly likely that they were encounters with the enigmatic Bracey. I once received a letter from a man named Henry, who lived in Wavertree in the late 1950s. Henry was a wife-beater and a drunk who became so violent, his wife up and left him and took their two children with her. Henry staggered from Yates's Wine Lodge one evening and caught a tram home from the stop on Brownlow Hill, next to Adelphi Hotel. Henry alighted from the tram on Picton Road, and, deciding he couldn't wait until he reached his home to answer the call of nature (from all the drinking) he went down an alleyway off Ash Grove, but was so drunk he collapsed and blacked out. Henry had a vivid dream of a man in a flowing cape coming down the alleyway. The figure wore a white wig of the kind worn by judges, and stranger still, this judge had a black mask with two eyeholes and a slit for the mouth. Henry was told by this masked stranger that he would die 'very soon' unless he stopped drinking. When Henry awoke in the lonely alleyway, he picked himself up off the cobbled floor and made his way home with the bleak warning from the uncanny Judge echoing in his mind. When he slept that night he had the very same dream, starring the masked magistrate all over again, and these dreams continued most nights until Henry eventually stopped drinking. It was a very hard, uphill struggle to stay away from alcohol, but in the end his perseverance paid off and he won back his wife and children and became a changed man who doted on them. In 1985, a 39-year-old Dingle man named Stephen developed a gambling problem. Each week he'd blow his wages in the bookies, and things became so bad he ended up robbing money from his mother's purse. One night, in February 1985, Stephen came home around 11pm from the pub in a drunken state to find that his mother had gone to bed. He noticed his mum's purse, carelessly left out on the dining table, and he opened it. He removed three tenners from the purse and then carefully closed it. Filled with guilt, he then turned on the television and tried to watch a programme to distract him from dwelling on his despicable theft. A soap opera called Falcon Crest was on the telly, and Stephen leaned back in the armchair and tried to watch it to avoid his conscience getting the better of him. Around 11.30pm Stephen dozed off and soon found himself in the midst of a terrifying nightmare. He was on trial in a gloomy looking mahogany-panelled court. The judge's face was just a black oval, and the twelve members of the jury were faceless and smooth as eggshells. A woman was called to the witness box to give damning testimony, and Stephen saw it was his mother. She told the court that her son had stolen money from her and then began to cry. 'I - I never dreamed the baby I once held in my arms would one day rob from me,' Stephen's mother sobbed. Stephen felt a lump of sorrow swell up in his throat. Then came a surreal, frightening sight. Stephen's mother left the witness box, and a group of pall-bearers – all faceless – carried a coffin into the courtroom. They stood it on end and put it in the witness box. The blank-faced judge told Stephen that the witness was his father. Stephen was very shocked and quite unnerved, because his father had been dead fifteen years. The coffin lid slowly creaked open, and Stephen's heart pounded away. The lid opened fully to reveal his father, in a state of decomposition, staring at him. One of his eyes slid, jelly-like, out its socket and down the grey bony cheek. Stephen tried to look away but he couldn't; he felt paralysed. His dead father told the court: 'He stole money from me when he was fourteen so he could buy a bike.'

Stephen recalled the shameful incident, way back in 1960, when he pilfered the money from his dad's wallet while he was asleep. 'I'm sorry,' Stephen said over and over again, until a man nailed the lid of his father's coffin shut. The pallbearers returned and took the 'witness' away.

The judge put on a black cap and sentenced Stephen to death, and the faceless pallbearers approached with an empty coffin. They seized Stephen and laid him in the coffin. He couldn't move an inch, and he watched them put the lid on the coffin. Then came the deafening heart-stopping sounds of the lid being nailed down by hammers. Silence then invaded the pitch-black pine box. Strange music was heard, and Stephen suddenly heard a faint roaring sound outside the coffin. The temperature started to rise, and smoke assaulted his nostrils. 'Oh my God, they're cremating me!' he muttered, and tried to get up, but there wasn't enough space. He gasped for air, but it was too hot and smoky to breathe. 'No!' he screamed.

And then he woke up. The heat was from the gas fire, which he'd left on maximum heat before dropping off, and the funereal melody he'd heard was the closedown music from the television. All the same, the nightmare had shaken Stephen to his marrow, and he put the thirty pounds he'd stolen from his mother back into her purse.

On the following day he went to visit a friend in West Derby, just to get himself away from the lure of his local betting shop in the Dingle. Stephen got off the bus on Muirhead Avenue and saw a bookmakers shop a little distance away. He felt an urge to use the only money he had – his return bus fare – to place a bet, but a funeral hearse passed by, followed by a cortege of black limousines, and Stephen's blood ran cold as he recalled the nightmare of the previous night. With the help of his friends and family, and with the ghastly memories of that dream of the creepy judge, Stephen successfully battled his gambling problem.

A psychiatrist would probably say that these so-called ghosts and nightmares are nothing more than manifestations of a guilt complex, but I have a feeling that the truth is much more sinister than that.

Perhaps the masked judge is still on his circuit, and maybe *you* will be appearing before him tonight...

THE GHOST OF DAVID ECCLES

Ghosts have an uncanny knack of teaching you all about the dark side of local history. In the late 1990s, the glowing spectre of a boy of about 8 or 9 years of age was seen in the basement of a certain building on Victoria Street. A woman working in the building saw the apparition close up and said there was blood coming from the child's ears, and he was also sobbing. A so-called medium was called in and claimed the boy had died in the Blitz. The clairvoyant also said he sensed that the spectral boy's name was John. I asked the medium if he could provide a surname, which would be of enormous help in identifying the boy when I consulted various archives and records. The medium grimaced and said he couldn't get the ghost's second name. I'm suspicious about self-proclaimed mediums who can only get a first name of a spirit and not the surname; surely if a first name comes through, it doesn't take much more effort to get the surname? I knew of a 60-year-old woman named Barbara who was genuinely psychic, and brought her to the haunted basement. Immediately she told me the boy's name wasn't John at all, but David, and she said he spoke in a Lancashire accent. He had not died in the Blitz as the other 'medium' claimed, but had been murdered well before World War Two, back in Victorian times. 'He's got no clothes,' Barbara told me, with tears in her eyes. Thanks to this and other information supplied by Barbara, I pieced together the following tragic tale.

On Sunday, September 6, 1891, Mary O'Brien, the mother of Robert Shearon, her eight-year-old 'illegitimate' problem child, decided that the only way she could stop her wayward boy from sneaking out of his Liverpool home at night was to deprive him of his clothes. Robert found a way round this predicament by cutting three holes in a sack for his arms and head, and he sneaked out of the house after dark. Robert went in search of his older friend, 9-year-old Sam Crawford, and he formulated a wicked plan to obtain clothes for his associate. In Great Charlotte Street on the following day at 2pm, Robert met a boy his own age named David Eccles. David, the son of a foundry worker, was smartly dressed in fine clothes, and he wore a cap and a pair of new well-polished boots. Like Robert and Sam, he was also playing truant that afternoon. Robert introduced his new acquaintance to Sam, and they walked off towards Victoria Street, where the two street-wise children took the naïve-looking David through a hoarding which surrounded an unfinished building. Robert and Sam called this place the "Rafts" because of the huge foot-deep pool of rainwater that filled the basement. There were a few children already playing on the building site, but as soon as these "witnesses" left, several hours later, Robert and Sam made David walk along an iron girder 12 feet above the pool. The boy was too scared to walk across, and Sam and Robert decided to push him off it. He landed with a splash, badly bruised. The sadistic duo made David get up onto the girder again and once more pushed him off. They stripped him of his clothes and boots as he came out of the water. Then they took him even higher up the building, onto a ledge, and then pushed him again. This time David Eccles hit the shallow pool and didn't get up, and to make sure he was dead, Sam Crawford knelt on his head as he lay under water. The two children watched the body for two hours, "to see if it moved" then divided the spoils. They dried the murdered boys wet clothes on a street brazier, then Robert Shearon went home.

On the following day, a group of boys were playing football on a piece of wasteland on Stanley Street, when one of them kicked the ball over the hoarding in Victoria Street. One of the kids went to get the ball, and he found the naked body of David Eccles, lying in a foot of rainwater in the basement pit. Initially, the police thought the unknown boy had drowned whilst bathing, but when Robert's mother read of the tragedy in the newspapers, and learned about the clothes of the child being unaccounted for, she realised where her son had obtained his new shirt and boots, and she went to the police. The parents of the murdered boy also became distraught when they heard about the finding of the child's naked corpse, and naturally thought the worst, because their boy had not returned home on the Monday. They later identified the body.

Robert Shearon made a full confession, as did Sam Crawford. In Court, the heads of the children barely reached the level of the dock, and they giggled as they gave their damning testimony, as if they didn't realise the enormity of their crime. The jury returned a verdict of "Wilful murder" against both prisoners, but the boys were acquitted on account of their youth. The tearful mothers of the children consented to the boys being sent away to a home.

WHEN THE DEVIL GOES TO CHURCH

In August 1886, a Catholic priest performed an impromptu exorcism on a 36-year-old bound and gagged woman named Bridget McGovern in the Liverpool Workhouse on Brownlow Hill. The priest, wearing a long black ankle-length cassock, recited these words: 'I command you, every evil spirit, in the name of God the Father Almighty, in the name of Jesus Christ His only Son, and in the name of the Holy Spirit, that, harming no one you will depart from this creature of God, and return to the place appointed to you; there to remain forever.'

Mrs McGovern, a pious, regular churchgoer from nearby Walnut Street, had, on the Saturday morning of 28 August 1886, walked into St. Philip Neri's Catholic Church, which stood, in those days, on Maryland Street, just around the corner from Rodney Street. Fifteen minutes before Mass was due to commence,

Bridget stood before the altar and began to take off her clothes. Mrs Walsh, the church cleaner, entered the holy building and saw Mrs McGovern stretched out naked on her back, on the aisle in front of the altar rails. She outstretched her arms and folded her legs, placing one foot on the other as if she was trying to mimic Christ on the cross, and this rude, revolting scene prompted the cleaner to take off her coat, rush down the aisle to cover the naked blasphemer. Bridget McGovern seemed dazed and insensible, but Mrs Walsh persuaded her to put on some of her clothes. The cleaner then hurried out of the church and attracted the attention of PC Colville 840, who had just turned into Maryland Street from Hope Street on his beat. The policeman and the cleaner struggled to dress McGovern in a rather haphazard fashion, and then the sacrilegious 'streaker' was taken directly to the Cheapside Bridewell and locked up. Bridget then began to roar like an enraged lion in her cell, and when a startled sergeant went to see who was making such a loud racket, he got the shock of his life. The face of the prisoner in the holding cell had changed from being elfin to evil. Her mouth was open, impossibly wide, and her protruding tongue was long, narrow - almost reptilian. It took four policemen to subdue Bridget, and to one of her uniformed restrainers, she made shocking accusations about him having an adulterous affair, and even named the woman he was allegedly seeing. The policeman seemed both astonished and horrified, and for a moment he unwittingly let Bridget's arm slip from his grip. She slapped his face and sent him reeling across the cell into the wall. Bridget was handcuffed and an old prison padre who happened to be visiting a friend at the Bridewell recognised signs of demonic possession in the woman, whom the sergeant described as a 'drunken disgrace' even though there wasn't an aroma of alcohol about her. The padre strongly advised the police to take the 'troubled lady' to a priest's house near to the Workhouse, but a Dr Cavanagh examined Bridget McGovern and said she was suffering from mental depression and a drink problem. Then Bridget began to speak in a mixture of Latin and Hebrew, and her words were recognised by the padre. She said she was host to one of the millions of fallen angels.

At the workhouse, a priest who was never identified had Bridget tied to a table and gagged to prevent her from frightening the few laymen present with her knowing remarks about their innermost secrets and fear. It is said that, during the five-hour-long exorcism, a pointed tail was seen protruding from under the priest's cassock, giving the impression that he was Devil himself, but he assured those witnessing the expulsion of the evil spirit that it was all a trick of the 'Foul Fiend'. The tail writhed and then withdrew back into the cassock. At one point a colony of black sewer rats poured out of a hole in the corner of the room and began screeching and leaping at those present, including the exorcist, and although he told his secular assistants to ignore the rodents, two people ran out of the room in fear. At the end of the Rites of Exorcism, a tall shadow of a man appeared on the wall, and then faded after a few moments. Moments later the sweet smell of violets pervaded the room.

Bridget was taken to the Workhouse Asylum for a while, where she made a quick recovery, and within a month she was once again attending Mass at St Philip Neri's on Maryland Street. The Liverpool Mercury newspaper picked up on part of the story, but the full scope of the incident was known only to a few priests and the jailers of the Bridewell for many years.

There have been other alleged possession cases in Liverpool churches. I remember one case in the 1960s when a devout female churchgoer startled the congregation in St Anthony's on Scotland Road one Easter by crying out a stream of profanities before collapsing. Everyone who knew the elderly lady were dumbfounded, and when she was taken to hospital, she regained consciousness and said all she could remember was a hot breath at the nape of her neck, then she passed out.

The *Liverpool Albion* newspaper records how, one Sunday afternoon in November 1847, Mass at St Jude's on Montague Street (near the top of London Road) was disrupted by an outbreak of uncontrollable screaming among the congregation. The first person to scream was a poor man who had been occupying one of the free seats in the church. The Reverend McNeile halted his sermon and asked for the man to be taken to the Vestry room, but even there his screams could still be heard, so the man – by now branded as a maniac – was removed from St Jude's but could still be heard hundreds of yards away from the church, such was the power of his voice. No sooner had the congregation settled down when all of a sudden, a respectable female in the congregation let out an ear-piercing scream. She screamed several more times, fainted, and was taken into the Vestry room. Minutes later, a second lady in the congregation began to scream uncontrollably at the top of her voice, and had to be carried out of the building via the front entrance. The congregation took a while to settle down, and the Reverend McNeile prayed for the three people who had been inflicted with the strange mania, and he continued with the divine service. After the service, as they left St Jude's, many members of the congregation talked in hushed tones about the devil being to blame for the strange outbursts.

In the summer of 1851, a master shipwright named Daniel Roxburgh, of Grafton Street, Toxteth Park, became possessed by something. His friends and family instantly noticed the drastic change in his personality and behaviour. He spouted passages from the New Testament, screamed aloud and seemed to develop Herculean strength. Unusual loudness of voice and a huge increase in strength are signs of demonic possession. Roxburgh became convinced he was God, and stormed off to St Mark's church on Upper Duke Street to talk to the people directly and cut out the middleman – the Reverend Pollock. It was a Sunday, and Pollock was up in the pulpit, half an hour into his sermon, when Roxburgh – brandishing a heavy walking cane and an umbrella – entered St Mark's and sat for a while at the back of the church. The sexton, Mr Boyd, noticed Roxburgh was acting strangely, talking to himself aloud, and obviously seeking attention from the congregation. Roxburgh suddenly headed for the door, and the sexton was about to escort him out of the church, but then the demented man made an abrupt turn and hurried towards the pulpit. The Reverend saw him approaching and Roxburgh shouted something to him that was not understood. 'Who are you? What do you want?' asked Reverend Pollock.

'I am God Almighty!' was Roxburgh's blasphemous reply. He told the preacher to come down, then after waiting impatiently for a few moments, he ran up the steps to the pulpit as members of the congregation gasped with astonishment. The sexton and a few of the churchgoers went up the steps after him. It took eight people to restrain the disturbed man, such was his strength, and the Reverend Pollock told those who held Roxburgh down not to hurt him if possible. Roxburgh was taken to a police station on Seel Street where he was tied to a cart to prevent him doing any harm to himself or others. Roxburgh broke the cart apart and frothed at the mouth. Six policemen bundled Roxburgh into a carriage and transported him to the main Bridewell, where a doctor opined that the prisoner was suffering from a 'brain fever'. Roxburgh was taken to the Workhouse, and bound to a table by the ankles and wrists until he calmed down somewhat. He was afterwards committed to a lunatic asylum, and nothing more was heard of him.

In the 1930s, a middle-aged man named Mathews rushed up into the pulpit of St Francis Xavier's Church in Everton one Sunday and, pushing the priest aside, began to deliver a sermon in an unintelligible language – possibly 'tongues' – also known as glossolalia in the paranormal sphere. The man was overpowered and taken to the local police station, where he made a profuse apology for his outrageous behaviour. He told a detective that he lived on Everton Brow and had attended the church for years. About ten minutes after attending Mass, the man felt an uncontrollable urge to get up into the pulpit and was unable to resist the overpowering temptation. A priest from St Francis Xavier visited the disturbed man and blessed him. There were no further disturbances at the church.

MY RAGGED VALENTINE

The growler - a green lacquered four-wheeled horse-drawn carriage - trundled away from the crowds of love-struck men, young and old, who had waited impatiently in the wintry weather outside the Royal Court Theatre, just to get a glimpse of the beautiful twenty-six-year-old Madame Georgina Burns, one of the greatest operatic singers of her day. So great was her fame that James Joyce even mentioned her in two of his novels. The soprano had just given another electrifying performance in Meyerbeer's Robert the Devil and now on this glacial Friday of 10 February 1888, the prima donna's carriage threaded its way through the snow-ghosted streets, bound for her temporary home on St James's Road. Snowflakes stung the eyelids of an army of admirers on Rodney Street, and they surged en masse from the pavements into the icy cobbled road, startling the horses of Georgina's carriage.

The growler came to a halt and the fans crowded

around it. Someone tried the door of the vehicle, and Mrs Smith, the loyal maid seated next to Georgina, thrust her arm out to close the door, and then lunged towards the opposite window, where two medical students were clinging on to the side of the growler, in order to peep in at the object of their intense affection. They managed to open the door and there was a scuffle, during which the maid accidentally dropped her mistress's satchel, containing money and five-hundred pounds' worth of jewellery. However, no one noticed the velvet satchel fall from the growler into the slush-covered road beneath, as all enthralled eyes were fixed on Georgina. The driver realised that he had to extricate her from the situation as quickly as possible, or risk serious harm coming to his charge, so he cracked his whip and the carriage quickly rolled away. The crowd reluctantly parted and the object of their adoration was soon back at home and it was only then that Georgina realised that her satchel was missing. She thought it must have been stolen in the crush and notified the police at once.

Three ragged teenaged boys crossed Rodney Street later that evening in sluicing icy rain, and one of them, Johnny Hughes, spotted the satchel in the road and swiftly picked it up. He and his two mates, the miserable Ben 'Jolly' Rogers and Mickey Ryan, hurried to a derelict house on Pitt Street to examine their find and could not believe their luck when they discovered the contents of the satchel; a fortune such as they had never seen before. After much excited discussion, the trio agreed to hide the booty in the cellar, until it was safe to pawn it. Johnny, however, sneaked back into the house shortly after his friends had departed, and removed a sparkling diamond ring and two gold sovereigns from the satchel.

It would soon be Valentine's Day, and Johnny thought it was time to propose to Mary Moore, his sweetheart of just three weeks. Mary sometimes spoke to him in a strange tongue, which sounded like gobbledygook to Johnny's ears, as he did not realise that most people spoke Gaelic in Bridgewater Street, where Irish-born Mary lived.

On the way to Mary's house on Valentine's Day, Johnny passed Cranky Mackintosh, an old tramp, but a very well spoken one, who was dreamily gazing through a pawnbroker's window at the silk topper, opera cape and frock coat he had 'popped' (pawned that is) two years ago, just after his bankruptcy and subsequent divorce and then rapid descent into penury, the slums - and insanity. Feeling great sympathy for the vagrant with the pomegranate nose, and not appreciating the true value of a sovereign, Johnny gave him one of the golden coins, upon which Cranky picked him up, hugged the wind out of him, and marched straight into the pawnbroker's. He soon emerged dressed in his yesteryear togs, with a fine walking cane and top hat, but despite this, he was weeping.

Mary and Johnny kissed in the 'Old Delf (St James's Cemetery), which is where the ragged Valentine proposed. She eagerly gave her consent in both Gaelic and English, but the ring never reached her finger, because Davy, the older brother of Ben 'Jolly' Rogers, turned up just as Johnny was slipping it on to her finger and snatched it away from him. Davy Rogers eventually returned the ring, and the rest of the jewellery, to Georgina Burns and received the fifty pounds reward that had been widely advertised in the newspapers.

Of course, Davy Rogers never knew about the stolen sovereign, and that kept Johnny and Mary in sweets for quite some time!

There is a sad end to this old tale. Johnny discovered Mary in the arms of a much older man in Sefton Park one summer's day. The stranger was an Irishman named Duggan, a friend of Mary's uncle. Duggan was a deeply unpleasant character, but he had somehow mesmerised Mary Moore into falling in love with him. In his presence she only had eyes for him; it was as if a curtain came down and obscured everyone but her new love when he was near. Johnny Hughes begged her to stay with him, but she refused to even consider it, and she and Duggan later married and moved away to London.

Johnny Hughes never got over the loss of his beloved Mary; no other girl ever lived up to her. It is said that Johnny served his time as an apprentice baker a few years later at the Liverpool Vienna Baker, on Hardman Street, now known as The Fly in the Loaf pub. In those days, the bakery supplied all the principal hotels, restaurants and even the banquets given by the Prince of Wales, with high-quality Viennese bread.

One evening, whilst Johnny was working overtime at the bakery, he thought he heard whispering. Other workers heard it too, but it was difficult to pinpoint where it was coming from. During a tea break, Johnny went upstairs to the rest room, and there was Mary Moore standing in a corner, dressed in a long white gown. Her lovely face was bruised black and blue and her skin had taken on a deathly grey hue and was almost translucent, quite unlike her former peaches and cream complexion.

"I'm really really sorry," she groaned, and she reached out towards Johnny.

"Mary?" Johnny gasped. "Can it really be you?" He was unafraid, even though he sensed she was a ghost. His great love for her overcame any fear.

"I still love you, Johnny," Mary's wraith told him, in a voice filled with emotion, and before he could reply she vanished, leaving Johnny standing there alone in a tense and empty silence.

Johnny Hughes later discovered that Duggan had been a vicious wife beater and had made Mary's life a misery from the moment they got married. He had lost his temper one night at their Hampstead home and in a frenzied rage had struck Mary as she stood trying to placate him on the upstairs landing of their home. The fatal blow sent her reeling and she fell down a whole flight of stairs. The spinal chord in her neck was severed in the fall and her short life ended at the bottom of those stairs.

Johnny is said to have hanged himself on the Hardman Street premises when Mary's death, and the manner of her death, were confirmed to him by a priest, and for years afterwards, bakery workers often saw the swinging shadow of a hanged man on the wall in the upstairs room.

THE PELLEW STREET HORROR

From 1880 to 1883, Rebecca Solidyke, a widow in her forties, kept an infamous brothel at 44 Pellew Street, which once ran parallel to Copperas Hill. The premises of the Postal Sorting Office now stand on the spot where the house of ill-repute once existed in Victorian times, and in the summer of 1882, something took place in the vicinity of the brothel that has never been explained. Let me take you back in time to the horrors that unfolded that summer. From behind a blackened sandstone wall, pearl plumes of steam blossomed in the balmy air as the locomotive rumbled along the lines into Lime Street Station, bringing someone – or something – from God knows where to the restless city of river breezes and carboniferous smoke. Barefoot children climbed that sandstone wall on Pellew Street to gaze into the chasm far below; at the determined ferns sprouting from the sandstone walls of a sheer drop, and the silver tracks that led to a better life somewhere, gleaming in stark contrast to the gravel and dull stones packed between the wooden sleepers.

On a July day when the blue sky smarted upturned eyes, a stranger appeared on Pellew Street, a street of damned souls, many of them destined for a brief mention in the Coroner's Inquest column of the local newspaper. These were the people the upper classes called loafers; the low life, the great unwashed minions, the riffraff. Why in the world would anyone as well-dressed as the approaching stranger come to Pellew Street? Haggard toothless women were seated on their knife-worn doorsteps; grimy cherubs ran in circles taunting emaciated mongrel dogs with washboard ribcages. A solitary hollow-eyed man in his twenties who had long resigned himself to the midden-dump of wasted youth looked on at the outsider with a blank expression.

The tall broad-shouldered visitor wore a pristine bowler, and beneath its brim was a bush of curly russet hair and a thick uncultivated beard that framed his peculiar pink pig-like face. He carried a bulging canvas sack of the type that returning sailors carry home, and he headed to the dilapidated-looking house next door to the brothel. A key was turned, and the old green warped door opened with some difficulty, but closed firmly behind the foreigner to those parts. The venetian-red front door of the brothel opened to release a fairly satisfied client, and Rebecca Solidyke ventured out onto the doorstep with her pretty 20-year-old daughter Mary. They thought they had heard the front door of the empty house next to the brothel slamming. They returned to their home as ruined folk of the dismal street watched them with contempt.

That evening, as the last shafts of a persimmon sunset lent some beauty to Pellew Street, a Spanish sailor named Mr Byzanti paid a visit to the harlot's house. He was a regular visitor, but in drink he was prone to violent behaviour, and had once given Mrs Solidyke a black eye. On this occasion he was merry but not sodden drunk. He wanted to make love to Mary, but her mother told him he couldn't. A prostitute named Julia took Byzanti into an upstairs room, and the Spaniard smiled at Mary as he went up the stairs. 'Next time,' he told the young woman.

Mrs Solidyke's son Billy came into the house, and Mary quickly ushered him into his room; he'd never come home as late before; even though it was summer. The boy had his little fox terrier Vic with him, and with great difficulty it was carrying a huge rib. Billy said the man who had moved in next door was kind because he had given Vic lots of meat and that rib.

On the following day, Billy and Vic followed the man next door to the butcher's shop on London Road. He bought pork neck ends, pig's trotters, ribs, pigtails, offal, livers, kidneys, brisket, sheep's heads, and customers complained about the stranger buying up everything out the marble slab in the window. The thickset man with the rose pink face and cylindrical pig nose then enquired about sawdust, which surprised the corpulent rosy cheeked butcher and the queue of impatient customers. The man slapped gleaming coins Billy had never seen on the counter and the butcher's assistant carried a sack of sawdust to the house on Pellew Street.

That afternoon, the new resident of Pellew Street slipped out of the house and visited an iron mongers with Billy and Vic, and around 5pm he put a bowl of diced meat on his doorstep which the fox terrier ate in a furious fashion.

Mrs Solidyke thought the man next door was eccentric, and she told her son he was not to go near him or accompany him to town any more. The boy reluctantly obeyed his mother's wishes but Vic would sneak off each day in the late afternoon and wait at the neighbour's doorstep, tilting his head and flicking his ears about in expectation. The door would open slightly and a pink hand would be seen placing the bowl of diced pork or beef on the step.

Vic gradually became rather plump, and while Billy thought it was funny, his mother and sister didn't, so they went next door and Mrs Solidyke hammered on the knocker. The man never answered, so Mary, being the literate one of the house, jotted down a note of complaint and posted it through the neighbour's letterbox, telling him to stop feeding Vic.

One evening, about a week later at 11pm, there was a rat-tat-tat at the brothel door.

Julia answered, and saw the weird-looking neighbour standing on the doorstep. He wore a grey flat cap and a long dark coat. His face was grotesque, and when he smiled, it reminded Julia of the comical painted plaster pig face that adorned a butcher's shop window on Lime Street.

'Go away,' Julia told him, with a look of disgust.

The neighbour's smile vanished and he gritted his teeth.

'Go on, piss off or I'll call a copper!' the prostitute threatened.

He moved away but Mrs Solidyke came to the door to see why Julia was shouting, and when the latter told her who she was shouting at, Mrs Solidyke called the man next door back.

When she saw his face, she was repulsed yet unaccountably intrigued. She asked him if he wanted to come in and the man said 'Yes,' in a gruff voice.

Miss Solidyke took him into the back parlour, and sat on the edge of a double bed.

He stood by the fireplace for a while, as the head of the brothel questioned him. She wanted to know where he was from. 'The country,' he said, rather enigmatically. What was his name? He never answered, but instead started to take off the long coat. He was naked, except for the boots he wore.

He sat on the bed, next to Mrs Solidyke, and his bulk, landing on the mattress shook her. By the light of a single oil lamp, she could see how his body was as revolting as his face. He had long thick arms and legs, as pink as a carnation, and his chest and abdomen were covered in rolling folds of goose-pimpled fat. He still had his flat cap on, and he suddenly removed it to reveal something that made the prostitute shudder. He had a pair of small rounded ears on each side of his head, but not in the places where normal human ears would be. These ears were on the upper sides of his head, so he looked like some pig-human hybrid.

He suddenly turned and seized Mrs Solidyke, then sucked hard on her delicate white neck. Her face was forced into the cold flesh of his chest, and she found herself being steadily suffocated. She couldn't move because his strong thick arms entrapped her, so she bit into him. She imagined it was like biting into the flesh of a freshly-plucked goose. Her teeth broke his skin and a fat blubbery substance oozed out. There was a dull groan, and he released her. Mrs Solidyke let out a scream and fell off the bed, onto the floor, landing on her backside. She screamed again, and the beast got up and put on the flat cap and long coat. Mrs Solidyke became violently sick as she wiped the white fat substance laced with blood from her lips. As Mary arrived in the hallway she saw the shadowy neighbour opening the front door. By the time the girl had gone to her mother's aid, the client had vanished.

Mary saw her mother's bruised neck, and a pool of vomit on the carpet. Mrs Solidyke gave an incoherent account of what had just taken place and her daughter suggested calling the police. Her mother threw up again and told her to forget the incident. The policemen she knew would never follow up a complaint from a brothel-keeper, and who would believe the bizarre description of the attacker anyway?

Days later, in the afternoon, as Julia was entertaining a customer, a rhythmic tapping sound was heard next door. It was constant, and occasionally became louder. The annoying racket continued throughout the day, and at 5pm, when the Spanish client, Mr Byzanti arrived at the brothel, Mary told the sailor about the assault and the strange physiology of the next-door neighbour. The Spaniard believed he'd have a good chance at making love to the delectable Mary if he went and sorted out the neighbour, and so he went next door and hammered on the knocker. 'Cerdo!' he shouted, which is Spanish for 'pig', and after getting no reply, he began to kick the door in.

At this point, young Billy arrived home and told his mother he couldn't find Vic anywhere. Mrs Solidyke brushed her son aside and went outside to see Mr Byzanti in action.

The sailor from Tarragona managed to kick the door open, and he took an ivory-handled dagger from a special sheath in his boot and stormed the house. A gaggle of enthralled children stood on the doorstep, watching Byzanti walk into the kitchen of the house. Their noses were greeted with an awful aroma; a mixture of rotting eggs and the odour of blood that hung in the air - very reminiscent of the butcher's shop. Bluebottles flew blindly out of the smelly house, striking the faces of the kids.

The 'pig-man' stood in the kitchen, wearing a blood-streaked apron. He held a chopper in his hand. The sawdust on the floor had soaked up quite a quantity of blood. The sailor saw dogs and cats, many without heads, hanging from meat-hooks that had been fixed to the kitchen ceiling. A pool of blood was still widening out from a diced dog on the kitchen table. To the horrified Spaniard's eyes, it looked like the remains of the terrier Vic.

The sailor ran at the abomination in the apron, and it swung the chopper downwards at him, intending to cleave his head open, but instead taking Byzanti's left ear clean off. Just the hole of his auditory canal remained where the ear had been, and blood slicked down his neck into his collar. In shock, the Spaniard lunged at the freak with the dagger, and its blade plunged deep into its chest. The hybrid squealed just like a pig, and blood sprayed everywhere. It turned and fled, and the Spaniard slipped in the bloody sawdust, and landed on the floor in agony, ready to pass out. There is an uncertain end to this horror story. Some accounts say the porcine hog-featured creature fled bleeding heavily down the warren of alleyways, pursued by a pack of ravenous dogs until it was torn to shreds by the hounds in Bronte Street. Other say the trail of the pig-like man's blood led to the nearby abattoir on Trowbridge Street, where a group of slaughterrmen cornered the freak, killed it, chopped it up, and fed the parts to the hungry canines.

Mrs Solidyke told the police about the 'man-beast' next door when they found the remains of the butchered animals, but she was right – the officers of the law did not believe her and looked at her condescendingly as nothing more than a low whore. On a happier note, when the police searched the cellar of the house next door to the brothel, a little dog was found locked in a crate. It was Vic, and once released, he yelped, lumbered to get his little portly frame up the cellar steps, and darted to his master, Billy, who was very pleased to be reunited with the fox terrier. The brothel was closed by the police in the following year, and Mrs Solidyke turned to alcohol and drank herself into an early grave in the autumn of that same year.

Any attempts to explain the taxonomical nature of the beast that moved into Pellew Street always fall flat. Surely some light would have been thrown onto this mystery if the police had discovered the identity of the tenant of the house next door to the brothel, because the man – whatever he was – possessed a key to that house, but in the absence of any concrete information, it's probably useless to speculate on this matter –

however, I'll never be able to look at a pig's head in the window of the butchers in the same way again.

A MESSAGE FROM MR SMITH

One windy March evening, at one minute to six, a middle-aged man named Raymond was sitting by himself, drinking in the Philharmonic Pub on Hope Street. He was expecting Lisa, his wife of ten years, to join him at any minute, for they had arranged to meet up at the pub when she finished work at her office in the city centre. Lisa was a business development manager, and usually left work at about half-past five, unless she had a special job on and was asked to work late, in which case she would normally tell Raymond in advance.

Raymond was becoming increasingly edgy; he instinctively felt there was something wrong. It was a cold heavy feeling in the pit of his stomach, which he had felt once before when ... oh, surely it couldn't be history repeating itself? His mind jumped back two decades, to the days when he was seeing Dawn, and how, just a few months after they became engaged, she abandoned him without a word of explanation. That same horrible feeling in the pit of his stomach had foretold that break-up and now here it was all over again. He told himself not to be so melodramatic, after all, Lisa was only a bit late, for which there could be a hundred and one perfectly innocent explanations - and yet Raymond could not think of one as he sat nervously jingling the change in his left trouser pocket and supping the remains of his copper-coloured bitter. He glanced at his watch at least once a minute, and then at his mobile phone, hoping to see a missed text message, or call. At 6.10pm, the mobile finally chimed out its ridiculous polyphonic melody. He had a text and he prayed that it was from Lisa, but it was only a special offer from his mobile network operator and he swore in frustration, the profanity drowned out in the hubbub of the pub.

At 6.30pm he couldn't stand it any longer and he rang Lisa, but only reached her infuriatingly jolly mobile answering service. He hung up immediately. At last, at 6.45pm, Lisa finally appeared, and apologised profusely for being so late. She had bumped into an old friend on Renshaw Street and they had had a quick natter and a drink in the Dispensary pub.

"Oh," was all Raymond could manage, as he wondered to himself why she had switched off her mobile and not bothered to ring him, but he said nothing. Because of a back injury, Raymond had been unable to work for a while, and so, on the following day, at around 2pm, he was to be found, as he often was, sitting in his semidetached home in Aigburth, twiddling his thumbs with boredom. He hated having nothing to do and the time dragged by so slowly until Lisa came home from work. He decided to check his e-mails. With a tired grimace he deleted the usual annoying spam and was mildly surprised to see an e-mail from a John Smith that addressed him by his first name in the subject part of the e-mail. It read, 'Raymond, I have news for you'.

Raymond naturally assumed that some online form he had filled in had been illegally shared by the usual unscrupulous data collectors of the Internet. Then he opened the e-mail and its stark first sentence instantly reignited those feelings of deep unease about his wife that he had experienced the day before: 'Raymond, I have news about Lisa. Something is going on that you should know about ...'

The rest of the message advised Raymond to leave a ten-pound note on top of the cold water cistern of a certain pub toilet that night at 7pm. The sender of the e-mail would then tell him something about Lisa that would be a shock, but would, at least, open his eyes to a terrible truth.

Raymond re-read the upsetting message several times before he noticed the address of the sender: stendec@mail.com. He e-mailed 'John Smith' with a query: 'Who are you?' No reply came back.

By 5pm, Raymond had made up his mind. It could be a hoax, but what if it was not? He telephoned Lisa and said he was going to see his aunt Margaret in Crosby, as she was poorly. He would be back at about half-past seven. Lisa was puzzled and said she had not been aware that he even had an Aunt Margaret, but Raymond told her not to be so paranoid and suspicious and promised to be back as soon as he could. Lisa called him again a little later on, and was irritated to find that his mobile was switched off. She was now even more suspicious and when she got home she called Raymond's sister Deborah, in Newcastle, and asked her if she had an Aunt Margaret. "Not as far as I know," Deborah laughed. "Why do you ask?"

"Oh, nothing, just Raymond's idea of a little joke," said Lisa and then quickly changed the subject. After she had put the phone down, she made herself a cup of tea and sat mulling over what had happened. Her husband was an amateur liar, and had never been a man who could cover up his tracks with a plausible story, which, in a way, she thought, was a good thing.

At 6.30pm, Raymond entered the pub where he was to put a tenner on the toilet cistern. It was a very small place, and very intimate. The petite red-headed barmaid smiled at him and raised her cherubic face in query. He asked for a medium coke with ice, because he had driven to the place and intended to drive back home. He thought it would look odd if he went straight to the toilet, so first he sat down in a corner and drank most of his drink. He then sauntered over to the gents to check it out, trying to look as casual as possible. There was only one cubicle, and there was the water cistern above it. He closed the cubicle door, stood on the seat, and felt the top of the tank, just in case it was open. It had a smooth flat roof. Raymond got down, without leaving the ten pound note on the cistern, since it was not yet seven o'clock, then left the cubicle, washed his hands and returned to the bar.

There were only three customers in the place, so which one was John Smith? A man of about sixty, wearing an old tweed jacket, pea-green trousers and brown brogues was straining his neck to look up at the television set on the wall, but by the sad faraway look in his eyes, he was not paying the blindest bit of attention to the programme. Surely he was too old to even send an e-mail? Raymond thought. Most of the people he knew of that age didn't know one end of a computer from another.

He then turned his attention to the next 'suspect' - a young man with a shaven head, wearing a Metallica tee shirt, who had a bottle of Budweiser on the table in front of him. Nevertheless, he was the number one suspect so far. Being young, he was probably very well-versed in computers and e-mails. How old was he exactly? - about twenty - Raymond reckoned, but then how would he know about Lisa, and how on earth would he have got hold of Raymond's e-mail address? So many unanswered questions, and it was now twenty minutes to seven. The third suspect was a woman of about forty, with a flushed complexion. She was drinking a pint of what looked like bitter. Not very lady-like, thought Raymond, in his usual chauvinistic way, and took another sip of his coke.

"John Smith," said the pint-drinking woman, out of the blue, and Raymond went cold, as he heard the name of the anonymous e-mailer actually voiced out loud. He scrutinised the woman, looking for clues, and felt his heart palpitating uncomfortably inside his chest. He was definitely not cut out for this kind of cloak and dagger stuff.

The woman suddenly noticed him staring, and smiled at him. "Okay love?" she said, in a slurred voice, and Raymond nodded, uncertainly. Then he noticed the barmaid filling a pint glass with John Smith's extra smooth bitter. He felt so ridiculous. He nodded back to her with a smile, and to avoid further eye-contact with the tipsy woman, he tried to enter into conversation with the cheerless individual who seemed to be lost in his own thoughts. "Windy out there tonight, isn't it?" Raymond began, rather weakly.

"Is it?" answered the man, his eyes still glued to the television set.

"Yes, blowing like a gale," lied Raymond.

"Is it?" the man reiterated.

"Yes."

This was one conversation that was obviously going nowhere and Raymond gave up, and also resorted to idly looking up at the television set.

The youth suddenly switched off his iPod and went to the toilet. Raymond lost no time in enquiring about this fellow. He said to the barmaid, "That lad reminds me of someone. I'm sure I've seen him before somewhere, but I can't think where."

"Ryan?" said the barmaid, taking the five-pound note off the middle-aged woman and opening the till.

"Is that his name? Yeah, I hate that when you can't place someone," Raymond went on.

The barmaid handed the change to her customer then said, "Yeah, I know what you mean. He's at uni somewhere ... nice lad."

It's got to be him, Raymond decided, but he was still left with the puzzle of how such an unlikely character had found things out about himself and Lisa.

After a minute or two, Ryan came back from the toilet and picked up a copy of a tabloid newspaper that was folded on the bar. As he started reading it, Raymond could not stop himself from asking, "Do you happen to know anyone called Lisa, mate?"

Ryan looked up from the page, "What?"

Raymond repeated the question and looked him straight in the eye. The barmaid was about to pull open a bag of peanuts, but she stopped, seemingly intrigued by the conversation that was unfolding between the two customers.

"Lisa who?" asked Ryan, looking at Raymond, puzzled.

Raymond almost smiled, "I just thought you might er ... know her ... or maybe John Smith."

Ryan shook his head once, and smiled in a sarcastic way, then looked at the barmaid and went back to flipping through the pages of the newspaper. Raymond suddenly had the feeling the he had got it all wrong. The boy looked too vacant to be the John Smith he had been piecing together in his mind. "Sorry, mate," he told Ryan, "I just thought you were someone else for a minute; I'm losing it."

As his watch ticked towards seven o'clock, Raymond again made his way into the pub toilet. The depressed drinker with no conversational skills was already occupying the only cubicle, so Raymond went over to the sink and washed his hands to kill time. As the hand dryer clicked off, he heard a snoring sound coming from the cubicle.

"Oh, my God! This is unbelievable," he muttered, and rapped loudly on the cubicle door. As he was doing so, Ryan came in and looked condescendingly at Raymond, as if he thought he was some kind of madman, or weirdo, then went over to the urinal.

"He's asleep in there!" Raymond complained to the young man, who didn't make any response.

Raymond then went and told the barmaid about the

drinker who had fallen asleep on the toilet and she grinned, as if it was a big joke.

"It's not funny. Can you get him out of there, please?"

"And exactly how am I meant to do that?" asked the barmaid.

Raymond let out a loud sigh of impatience and barged back into the toilet, where he could now hear the man crying inside the cubicle. He passed Ryan on the way in, and the lad was smirking to himself.

Raymond was usually a mild-mannered man, who rarely swore or raised his voice, but he now found himself hammering on the cubicle door and cursing loudly. After a few seconds there was a small click, then the door opened and the man in the tweed coat came out, dabbing his eyes with a handkerchief. Raymond barged past him into the dark enclosure of the cubicle, slammed the door and fastened the bolt. He looked down into the toilet bowl and saw a crumpled length of toilet paper. He then took the ten-pound-note from his wallet, stepped on the toilet seat, and looked over the cubicle door to check whether any witnesses were loitering there, but he was alone. He folded the tenner and placed it carefully on top of the cistern.

Before he left the pub, he eyed all three customers again for one last time and as he went out of the door, the barmaid called out, "Bye."

He knew that he would have a lot of explaining to do when he reached home, and as he drove down Aigburth Road a peculiar question jumped into his mind. Could John Smith actually be Lisa herself, somehow testing him out, or playing some kind of joke on him? What a twist in the tale that would be. No, he dismissed the suspicion from his mind, telling himself that he needed to get a grip.

As soon as he walked through the front door, Lisa asked him how his Aunt Margaret was, and he immediately suspected, from the tone of her voice, that she had already checked out his story by calling his sister in Newcastle. "She's dead," he quipped.

"That's really not funny, Ray. Where have you been?" Lisa seemed concerned, or possibly suspicious of his antics.

"Okay, I'll tell you the truth. I drove up to Southport, just to get away from these four walls for a while. I just needed to get out and get some fresh air. Is that a crime?" he asked her, with a remarkable degree of faked sincerity in his voice and eyes.

Lisa eventually believed him, and later on, she confessed to thinking the worst - that he was having an affair. "What a hypocrite!" he thought, but he kissed her anyway and then went to check his e-mails in his study. He spotted John Smith's unopened e-mail immediately and clicked on it. It opened, and the unsigned message read: 'Raymond, Lisa has been seeing a man named Oliver Jones. She met him at the Pan American bar in January and has been seeing him twice a week ever since.'

Raymond felt that cold metallic sensation in his stomach taking hold again. He went to bed that night, and in the darkness, as he lay beside his wife, he asked her if she was awake.

"Yes, why?" came the reply.

Raymond felt so choked up, he could barely speak for a few moments, and he concentrated hard on the bedside clock's luminous green fingers as he tried to compose himself. "Who's Oliver Jones?" he managed to ask her at last.

The only sound for a while was the bedside clock ticking away the night-time seconds of eternity.

"Who told you?" asked Lisa, eventually. It didn't even sound like his wife's voice. It was emotionless and flat.

Raymond reached out and switched on the bedside lamp, pouring truthful light on the deception. "Never mind who told me. What's going on?"

Lisa turned away and buried her face in the cool soft cotton pillow. Her muffled sobs told Raymond all he needed to know and confirmed that John Smith's information had been genuine. It was crazy, but his mind then wandered off at a tangent. Shock affects us all in different ways, and instead of perhaps reflecting on how the affair would threaten his ten-year marriage, Raymond found himself wondering about two things: who was John Smith? and why had he only asked for a paltry ten pounds in return for this, to him, earth-shattering piece of information?

Lisa eventually got up, stepped into her slippers and put on her dressing-gown. She wiped the tears from her eyes and seemed to be bracing herself to say something.

"Where are you going?" Raymond asked, listening to his own hollow voice as if it belonged to someone else. Then suddenly, all the pent-up emotion of the last two days welled up inside him and he started shouting at her and calling her all the obscene names he could think of. Once he had started, he could not stop himself. He was like a man possessed.

Lisa just stood there calmly, waiting for the storm to subside. She had already made up her mind and just allowed the tirade of words to wash over her. Eventually, Raymond stopped shouting and seemed to shrink back into himself, like a deflated balloon.

"I'm leaving you, Ray," she told him, taking advantage of the lull, and then headed for the door.

Lisa went downstairs and sat in the kitchen for a while, smoking a cigarette. After about five minutes, a shell-shocked Ray followed her down. She told him that the affair with Oliver had just started as a fling, a bit of fun, and she had fully intended to end it after a week or two, but now she had come to realise that she should have been with someone like Oliver years ago. Their marriage was dead. Dead as a coffin-nail.

Raymond cried and cried and begged her to stay, but all his pleadings fell on deaf ears. Later that morning, at first light, she left in a taxi and that was the end of that. A day or two later she sent her sister round to collect her clothes and personal belongings. The loss of his wife in such a cold and final way left Raymond feeling deeply shocked and depressed, and then of course, there followed the painful and protracted divorce saga. For Raymond, it was a living hell.

Six months later, he was sitting watching television one afternoon, in a very depressed state, when his best friend Lawrence called at the sad empty house and persuaded him to join him for a drink. Raymond was not feeling in the least bit sociable, but he eventually consented and he and Lawrence went to a few bars in the Lark Lane area and then visited the Everyman Bistro for something to eat. Lawrence was delighted to bump into John Leadbeater, an old teacher from his school, at the bistro, and he and Raymond shared a table with the elderly man.

Over a period of two hours they discussed life, politics, the pitfalls of the National Curriculum, sport, women, various television programmes, and finally, the supernatural. By the time this topic had arisen, the three men had moved into the bar area adjacent to the bistro, and had all progressed on to shorts. During the conversations about such things as ghosts, the Devil, weird coincidences and curses, Leadbeater mentioned something that sobered Raymond up in a flash. "Have you ever had an e-mail off the Devil yet?" Leadbeater asked, in a rather random fashion.

Lawrence and Raymond smiled, assuming that a witty punch line would follow the joke, but it soon became obvious that the old teacher was deadly serious. His earnest, magnified eyes darted from side to side through his spectacle lenses as he scrutinised the faces of the younger men to see if he was being taken seriously.

"An e-mail from the Devil? Whatever next?" laughed Lawrence and grinned uneasily, fearing his old tutor had succumbed to some ageing disease of the brain.

"About two years ago, I received an e-mail from a John Smith, asking me if I wanted to know who had shot my cat," Leadbeater continued, undeterred. Raymond's ears immediately pricked up and an icy tingle shot down his spine. That name - John Smith - all the painful memories came flooding back to haunt him, even through the alcoholic haze.

"My wife and I were devastated by the death of our pet. He was shot in the head with a .22 pellet, fired from an air rifle ... died instantly. Mr Smith said I was to leave a ten-pound note in a certain book," Leadbeater recalled, and struggled to remember the name of the book in question. "What was it now? Ah yes, Science, Music and the Self, by Joseph Hallam; a small dark paperback in the philosophy section of my local library. If I did this he would tell me who killed our pet.

"Well I did do it. I know it sounds naive and ridiculous. But I did it. A few days later I received an e-mail from Smith, naming the culprit: a fifteen-year-old boy called Kevin. His address was given in the e-mail, and I telephoned Crimestoppers and told them I had good grounds for thinking there were firearms at that address. The police investigated, and in Kevin's bedroom, they came upon a cache of pellet guns and high-powered catapults that fired ball-bearings. This lad Kevin confessed, claiming to have shot the cat by accident, and he said he was sorry. He had been firing randomly, and had hit the cat by accident. He had two cats himself and said he would never knowingly harm an animal. Everyone who knew the lad confirmed he was an animal lover.

"He wasn't charged, but the boy became alienated by all the bad publicity. He hanged himself last year, and I still feel ... in a way ... that it was my fault."

"No, of course it wasn't your fault, Mr Leadbeater. It was just one of those things," said Lawrence, in an attempt to allay his feelings of guilt.

In a low, almost whispering voice, Leadbeater said, "Afterwards, out of curiosity, I looked for that book in the local library - Science, Music and the Self - and couldn't find it anywhere. I checked the book catalogue, and couldn't find any reference to it.

Looked on Amazon ... no such book."

"What about John Smith's e-mail?' asked Lawrence. "Maybe that could be traced."

Leadbeater hiccuped and then coughed. He seemed to be lost in thought for a while, then finally he answered his former pupil's question. "It was a name, like Stendec," and I don't know how to trace IP numbers and all that. But I had the feeling it was from the Devil, that e-mail, because I discovered other people who had received similar e-mails, all with the same name ... John Smith."

"Actually, I received the exact same type of e-mail,' admitted Raymond, and he went on to tell them the whole story about the request by Smith to put the money on top of the cistern in the pub toilet.

"You check that pub out," said Leadbeater, peering over the rim of his glasses at Raymond. "I'll bet you anything it doesn't even exist."

"No, it existed alright," said Raymond, recalling it in every detail, but then he suddenly had a nagging doubt about it and decided he would pay a visit to the place in the morning, just out of curiosity.

On the following morning, Raymond still felt groggy from the prolonged drinking session, and so wisely telephoned a cab to take him to the pub where he had left the tenner on the toilet cistern. When he reached the building, he saw it did exist, but it was all boarded up, and when he looked through the gaps in the boards on the windows, it was plain to see that the interior was in a dreadful state of decay. He asked a few passers-by how long that pub had lain empty, and most of them said it had been like that for at least three years. In the end, he contacted the brewery that supplied the derelict pub with its ale, and was officially told that it had been closed and boarded up since three-and-a-half years ago.

A few days after this frightening revelation, another e-mail arrived in Raymond's Outlook Express inbox - from John Smith. It contained no message, just four strange characters, which look like a grinning horned face:

}:-)

THINGYBOB

All children are capable of seeing, hearing and feeling things that adults cannot perceive. Children also have thoughts that 'mature' minds would not entertain, because they seem silly, which is a pity, because this blinkeredness is the reason why so many adults live their lives in a rut. Ask a silly question, and you just might not get a silly answer (as the proverb promises), but maybe something as important as the cure for the common cold. Let the adults play their 'brain training' games on their little hand-held game consoles; let them think they're clever solving their Sudoku puzzles, whilst they miss out on a whole universe of extraordinary goings-on, which are happening right under their very noses. The following is a case in point in the form of a story I researched a while back.

In the year 2002, a family, we shall call them the Hargreaves, were living on Conleach Road in Speke - a road which has acquired quite a reputation amongst serious ghost-hunters and researchers into the paranormal, because a certain house there has a long history of hauntings. However, the Hargreaves did not live in that particular house on Conleach Road, but one rainy day in the middle of a typical English summer, the family's meandering stream of conversation turned to the subject of ghosts. No one knew how the talk turned to that subject but it did. Up until that point when the ghost stories started, little five-year-old Skylar Hargreaves had been sitting at her miniature desk on her little pink chair, blissfully drawing in the big sketch pad that Nanny Jo had bought her. Skylar's mum Michelle sat drinking a can of Coke, listening to her mother's engrossing tales about phantom footsteps, faces at the window and family pregnancies foretold in dreams.

"Are all ghosts naughty, Nanny?" Everyone turned towards Skylar. They had not realised that she was even listening and her innocent enquiry punctured the tense atmosphere.

"Oh my God! We shouldn't be talking about stuff like this in front of her!" Michelle leaned over to her daughter, patted her head, and then knelt beside the tiny desk to admire her drawing. She wondered what to say to allay any fear she might have from listening to the stories. "There are no such things as ghosts, Skylar," was all she could come up with. "Nanny was just pretending."

"But Nanny said there's a ghost down the road," Skylar's big eyes opened wide, and her little mouth formed into a circle as she waited for Michelle to explain that one away.

"She was just joking, love," her mother said and she looked at Skylar's drawing of a tall yellow rectangle with a teardrop shape at the top of it. In this teardrop there was a grinning face. "Who's that?" she asked, just for something to say.

"Well, Nanna had a candle and she lit it for me and Thingybob was in it," Skylar told her mum with an intense wide-eyed expression.

"Thingybob? Who's Thingybob?" Michelle asked, trying to keep a straight face.

"He's not a boy," said Skylar, with a look of displeasure, having sensed that she was not being taken seriously.

"Oh! So he's a girl then?" Michelle reasoned.

"No!" Skylar bawled, frustrated, and her Uncle Eric told her not to shout - it was rude.

"Well, what is Thingybob then?" Michelle asked, fascinated by her five-year-old's fertile imagination.

"He's my friend," Skylar proudly told her.

Nanny Jo filled in a few blanks, "Skylar had been mooching about in the cupboard under the sink and she found this old candle. She asked what it was and so I showed her. I lit it, and she said there was a face in the flame. The funny thing was, I thought I saw it as well."

"Saw what?" Michelle asked.

"A face," said Nanny Jo, and gave a chesty cough.

"Take no notice of her," interrupted Uncle Eric, "She's seeing things. I was there and I saw nothing."

"I wasn't seeing things," replied Nanny Jo, indignantly. "By the time you dragged yourself from the telly to have a look, it had gone."

Uncle Eric's mouth became lopsided and he shook his head dismissively.

Grandad Barry then came in to the living-room. He had just returned from the allotment, where he had had enough of the rain pattering on the greenhouse, stopping him from doing anything. He heard them talking about Thingybob, and, thinking he could whisper to the adults without Skylar hearing what he was saying, he started talking in hushed tones about some of the weird things he had seen when he was a child in Tuebrook, even though Michelle kept shaking her head at him to discourage him from talking in front of Skylar.

"You know what?" Grandad Barry said. "When I was a kid, me and me mates used to go down to Windsor Road when it was getting dark, and wait across the road from this old empty house, and we'd see an old woman in a rocking chair, knitting. She used to wave at us. Eric remembers this ... Don't you, Eric?"

Eric grunted something, then said, "She was probably a tramp squatting in the house, or something."

Grandad Barry slowly shook his head and closed his eyes. "She was no tramp, Eric. It was the ghost of the old lady who used to live in that house. If you were brave enough and you crossed the road to try and get a better look at her - like we did a couple of times - you'd just see this empty room with the ceiling beams showing."

"Can we change the subject please?" Michelle asked, and angled her head to look at the picture of

Thingybob Skylar had drawn. "Why don't you draw a house with some flowers round the door, love?" she asked her daughter.

"A haunted one?" laughed Skylar, her eyes all aglow with enthusiasm.

"No, just a normal one, Sky," her mother told her and shot an angry look at her father.

On the following afternoon, Skylar was playing in the back garden with next door's youngest lad, Charlie, aged eight. He was throwing a black and white beach ball at Skylar, and she was giggling furiously and punching it back at him. Michelle smiled as she watched the children playing happily through the kitchen window. She cast her mind back to the time when she was pregnant with Skylar. She had suffered a placental abruption, and were it not for the expert work carried out by the specialists at the hospital, she would have lost her. She traced the line of the faint scar from the Caesarean with her fingers. Charlie later left the garden when he was called home for his tea, leaving his beach ball behind. Skylar carried it into the house and stood looking at her mother with a concerned expression - Michelle recognised that look as the one she pulled when she had done something naughty and was worried about being rumbled.

The inflated ball was about sixteen inches in diameter, and Skylar could just about hold it, it was so big compared to her little arms and hands. As Michelle looked on, something very peculiar happened; something which still makes her shudder to this day, even just talking about it. The ball rapidly deflated - but not in the uneven, crumply way that a ball of that kind usually collapses when the air is let out. No, in an instant this beach ball shrank before Michelle's eyes, until it was only the size of a golf ball.

She stood there, puzzled for a few moments, and then Skylar dashed out of the kitchen holding the little black and white ball. Her mother ran after her and asked if she could take a closer look at the shrunken ball. Skylar shook her head defiantly and clung on to the ball, but Michelle prised the ball out of her hands anyway. She scrutinised it, and was surprised to find a smiling but eerie face embossed into the fabric.

"Is that Charlie's face?" she asked her daughter, who was now sulking, head down with a protruding bottom lip. She refused to answer her mum's question and asked if she could now have her ball back.

Michelle went next door after tea with the now tiny ball and asked Charlie if the incredible shrinking beach ball belonged to him. He said no, it was Skylar's. She had told him that she had found it in her bedroom. Charlie's mother asked if she could have a look at the ball, but when Michelle looked down, it had mysteriously disappeared from the kitchen table. Charlie looked under the table and all over the room, but it was nowhere to be found.

A week later, Michelle went down with one of the worst attacks of a summer flu in her life. She was confined to bed for over a week, and her husband Ian looked after her, along with her mother. One night, when she was delirious with a high temperature, she kept thinking she could see a shadow darting about her bedroom. She would doze off for short periods of fitful sleep which were always interrupted after a short time by violent fits of coughing, which would also wake up Ian beside her.

At 3am, Michelle awoke from a nightmare in which a man dressed all in black was climbing into Skylar's room through the window. She woke Ian up and asked him to go and check Skylar's bedroom, and he told her to try and get some sleep, as he had checked their daughter's room earlier and everything was fine. In a huff, Michelle said she would go and check it, if he couldn't be bothered, and so Ian reluctantly got out of bed, and went to check that everything was alright.

He was gone for quite a while, so Michelle shouted him. There was no reply. She panicked and shouted louder, which set her off coughing again, and then her husband returned and said that everything was fine; Skylar was sleeping soundly. The bedside lamp was switched off, the couple cuddled in the darkness, and then Ian mentioned something which set alarm bells ringing in Michelle's mind.

"Who got her that clock?" he asked, casually.

"What clock?" asked Michelle, trying to smother another painful burst of coughing. This flu was really taking its toll on her lungs.

"There's a clock on Skylar's wall with a funny face on it. I didn't notice it earlier. Did you buy it?" asked Ian sleepily, closing his eyes and exhaling deeply as he began to relax, ready to descend into a well-deserved slumber.

"A clock with a face?" said Michelle, suddenly alert. She switched on the bedside lamp with a feeling of foreboding.

"What now?" Ian cried, and opened his eyes yet again. He squinted in the lamplight glare as he turned to face his wife.

"You said there was a clock with a face on," said

Michelle, remembering the face on the beach ball. She felt a cold shiver of unease, and it wasn't from the flu.

Ian swore, sat up, and said, "So what? Lots of kids' things have pictures of faces on them; Mickey Mouse, Donald Duck ..."

Michelle got out the bed. She felt dizzy, and reached out to steady herself on the wardrobe.

"Where the bleedin' hell are you going now?" Ian asked.

"To have a look at something ... there is no clock on Skylar's wall," said Michelle and she tottered unsteadily to the door.

Ian was close behind, "Are you sure you're feeling alright?" he asked. "You should be in bed," and he followed her into Skylar's room, worried that she might pass out at any minute.

There was no clock, with or without a face, on the wall, just the usual Winnie the Pooh alarm clock on the cabinet next to their daughter's bed. Ian was dumbfounded. He swore that he had seen a black and white clock on Skylar's bedroom wall. He examined the spot where the clock had hung and saw, by the light shining in from the landing, that there was no hole where a hook or nail might have supported the absent smiling clock. He turned on the light in the bedroom so he could have a better look, and Skylar moaned a little in her sleep, but her mother stroked her head reassuringly and she did not wake up. The wall was perfectly smooth.

Back in their bed, the couple lay in the darkness. "I was half asleep when I went into the room," said Ian, desperately trying to justify the clock's absence, "so I might have been seeing things."

Michelle then told him about the black and white beach ball that had shrunk before her eyes, and how it too had had a strange face on it. He asked her to describe the face.

"It had really prominent round cheeks, a smiling mouth, and two eyes that were like crescent moons turned on their side," she recalled. Ian suddenly felt very ill at ease, because that was exactly how he remembered the face on the clock in Skylar's room. "Was the nose totally round, like a little button?" he asked.

"Yes!" exclaimed Michelle, "I forgot to mention the nose. That's exactly what it was like."

The two of them lay there, holding hands, now fully awake. They were both lost for words.

A few days later, Ian had to work nights for a week, which made life rather difficult, because Michelle was still very poorly and unable to look after Skylar. Michelle's mother would usually have stepped in to help, but she was coming down with the same flu that was afflicting her daughter. Her father and uncle both made excuses and said they could not mind Skylar and help out in Ian's absence, so Michelle was in a bit of a fix. Fortunately, Ian's fifteen-year-old cousin Selina, who lived on nearby Woodend Avenue, kindly volunteered to help out. She knew nothing about the strange goings-on with the shrinking beach balls and the vanishing wall clocks and Michelle had no intention of telling her about these weird incidents - it might put her off coming.

Skylar loved Selina, especially when the teenager arrived with some sweets, because she loved spoiling Skylar. Around 7.30pm on the evening Selina came over to help, Michelle went to bed feeling exhausted, and asked Selina to put Skylar to bed around 8pm. At a quarter to eight, Selina was sitting on the sofa with Skylar in her arms, looking at the television. She happened to glance to her right, and noticed an oddly-shaped lamp, on a small round coffee table, to which she took an immediate liking.

Selina was a Goth; she wore pale make-up, heavy eyeshadow and mascara, and she yearned to dye her hair Tokyo Purple, but her schoolteachers would not allow it. The table lamp had a strange black silk shade that was shaped like a church bell. The neck and stand were matt-black and felt rubbery to the touch. Selina reached under the shade to locate the switch but there did not seem to be one. "That's funny," she muttered, "a lamp with no switch."

"That's not a lamp, silly" sleepy-eyed Skylar told Selina. "It's Thingybob."

Selina did not immediately realise what the little girl was saying. It was then that she noticed the smiling face imprinted on the funereal shade and thought it rather odd, although she did not pay it that much attention. She put the lamp shade down on the table and picked up the television remote to browse the channels.

A few minutes later, Selina noticed that the black lamp had gone - unaccountably disappeared without trace. She felt more than a little disturbed by the object's vanishing act and got up to turn on the ceiling light. No, it had definitely gone; there was no sign of it anywhere. Selina went upstairs and crept into Michelle's darkened bedroom. She was going to tell her about the black lampshade that had vanished, but as soon as she saw how pale and sick she looked, she decided to say nothing. Instead she asked, "Can I get you anything, Michelle?"

"Oh, I'd love a hot cup of tea, if that's okay, Selina," Michelle replied in a croaky voice.

"Sure, coming up!" Selina was just glad that Michelle was still awake, as the weird incident downstairs had made her feel very edgy.

"All I've done all day is drink tea ... I can't eat anything though," said Michelle dragging herself up to a sitting position and coughing into a handkerchief.

"I'll make you a pot of tea if you like," Selina suggested.

Michelle attempted a small chuckle and asked her if she knew how to brew a pot of tea, as Selina lived on soft drinks like so many of her generation.

"Of course, my tea tastes fab, Chelle," the girl promised, and went downstairs singing.

Down in the living-room, Skylar could be heard talking to someone. Selina entered the room and asked who she was talking to.

"Thingybob," said Skylar, gaily. "He was teaching me this really good rhyme and I was copying it."

Trying not to show her concern, Selina asked, "What rhyme was that then?"

In a barely audible self-conscious voice, Skylar whispered, "Star light, star bright, first star I see tonight, I wish I may, I wish I might, have the wish I wish tonight."

"That's very good." Selina crouched down to Skylar's level and hugged her, before picking the child up. "You'll have to go to bed soon, little one," she said. She carried the little girl into the kitchen and sat her down on the kitchen worktop, then half-filled the kettle and looked around for the teapot. She couldn't find it, so she asked Skylar if she knew where it was.

"Over there, under the tea-cosy," said the child, pointing to the table in the middle of the kitchen, where there stood a blue gingham tea-cosy, pointed like a Bishop's mitre.

"Oh, yes. Silly me! Why didn't I see it there?" Selina pulled off the tea-cosy and nearly jumped out of her skin. The bulbous teapot had the usual swan-necked spout and ear-shaped handle, but it had no glaze to its surface. It was dull and black, and there was that same face again that Selina had seen on the lamp, only this time the round face was not smiling - far from it. It looked angry, with knotted eyebrows and a livid mouth and its nostrils flared in its button nose.

Selina backed away, speechless with disbelief. The mouth of the teapot then opened to reveal a set of yellowish discoloured teeth, and from out of this unlikely orifice a swear-word was emitted.

"That's Thingybob," said Skylar, unperturbed by her odd friend's sudden change of demeanour, and she introduced Selina to her friend.

Selina was having none of it and turned and ran out of the house faster than if it had been on fire, leaving the door ajar. Skylar's bottom lip protruded and a solitary tear trickled down her cheek. She waited with a sulky face for a while, in case Selina returned, but after fifteen minutes of waiting, she climbed the stairs to her mother's room to tell her what had just happened.

Michelle Hargreaves dragged herself out of her sickbed, put on her warmest coat, wrapped up her child, and telephoned for a taxi to take her to her mother's home in Garston. As she waited in the hallway for the taxi, she saw a matt black balloon hovering about in the living-room, so she closed the door on it. A Hackney cab pulled up ten minutes later, and Michelle locked her front door and carried Skylar out to the vehicle. As the cab pulled away, mother and daughter looked out of the taxi door window at the sinister black balloon hovering at the window, as if the thing were watching them.

Michelle gave Ian a harsh ultimatum when he tracked them down to her mother's the next morning - either they leave that house on Conleach Road immediately, or she was leaving him and taking Skylar with her. After Ian had heard about the strange incidents he was only too keen to move. The family found a new house in Childwall, and for a while, they were anxious that 'Thingybob' - whatever it was -might follow them, but thankfully they never saw the mysterious 'shape-shifting' entity again.

As Skylar grew older, she was able to give her parents more information about the uncanny entity. It was she who gave it the name 'Thingybob', after hearing her grandad use the word in conversation and liking the sound of it. Skylar told them how the thing would appear on the end of her bed on some nights, usually manifesting itself the size of a tennis ball. It had tentacles like a miniature octopus and two blue illuminated eyes that would pulsate rhythmically as it spoke. It talked in a low whispering voice, but she could not recall anything in particular that it had said, or even what it talked about. Being so young and unquestioning, Skylar had simply accepted the entity for what it was, and as it had never harmed her, she took it to be her friend.

Was that being extraterrestrial, or was it perhaps from some other dimension? Scarier still - could Thingybob still be around today?

SOME HAUNTED LIVERPOOL SHOPS

Many of the shops in the city centre - and quite a few in the suburbs for that matter - have their own resident ghosts. Marks and Spencers on Church Street is housed in a building that was once the Compton Hotel, built on the site of Compton House, a popular retail store run by Messrs Jeffrey, which used to make the impressive boast of being able to provide everything the shopper needed 'from the cradle to the grave'. Colossal in its proportions, Compton House was staffed by hundreds of men and women, many of them living on the premises.

At 10pm on the Friday night of 1 December 1865, two policemen on their beat in Tarleton Street noticed smoke issuing from the basement of Compton House, which was the shop's outfitting department. Within twenty minutes, a steam-powered fire-engine and a body of firemen were dispatched from the Fire and Police Station at Hatton Garden to fight the blaze. The live-in staff members were rescued and brought to safety by the firemen, but despite the gallons of water hosed on to the flames, the inflammable materials in the store were nigh on impossible to extinguish, and Compton House, which had begun life as a modest drapers in 1832, and had grown to unimagined proportions, was totally gutted.

How did such a devastating fire start in the first place? Well, it turned out that it was deliberately started by a character called Thomas Henry Sweeting, a twenty-year-old respectably-connected apprentice of Compton House, who had been present in the store on the night of the blaze. He had apparently gone down into the basement shortly before 10pm, and there had lit a wax taper, which he threw amongst what he knew to be some highly inflammable merchandise. He then calmly went upstairs to have his supper. Within minutes, he saw smoke gathering on the premises and raised the alarm, crying, "The house is on fire ... make haste for your lives!"

When interviewed, Sweeting claimed that he felt no animosity towards his employers, and could not provide the police with any motive for destroying Liverpool's greatest department store. "I must have been mad at the time," was the best explanation he could come up with, when brought before the magistrate at the police court. He certainly seemed unbalanced, and it was also found that he had stolen seventy-four pounds' worth of merchandise from the temporary store that his employers had set up at Newington.

Sweeting was charged with having unlawfully and maliciously set fire to Compton House, causing damage to goods and property valued in excess of two-hundred thousand pounds. He was also charged with larceny, and duly committed for trial, the upshot of which was that he was found guilty, and sentenced to twelve years' penal servitude.

Messrs Jeffrey never recovered from the actions of the madman Sweeting, and Compton House, once a magnificent grand emporium of trade, remained a charred eyesore on Church Street for a decade. Then phoenix-like, from that blackened rectangle of scorched ground, there arose, on 4 January 1875, the Compton Hotel. It occupied the block between Basnett Street and Tarleton Street, and expanded in size in the 1880s.

By 1926, 'the Compton' had closed its doors, and from around 1930, Marks and Spencer moved into a small part of the building, and, of course, this phenomenally successful business went on to expand until it occupied the entire former hotel.

It is not unusual for a building as old as the Compton Hotel to be haunted by a few ghosts, although many of them will remain unidentified. The upper floors of Marks and Spencer are allegedly haunted by a ghost nicknamed 'Lulu' who, from her attire, seems to date back to the 1930s. For some peculiar reason, she often materialises holding a soda siphon out in front of her, and has even squirted people with it before vanishing. This ghost has never been explained, and as far as I know, no medium has attempted to contact her.

Another entity who occasionally haunts the building may be the ghost of Billy McMullen, a twenty-two-year-old junior porter who suffered a tragic and violent death at the Compton Hotel, in March 1877. McMullen was messing about in the hotel's kitchen lift, which was little more than a suspended cage used for transporting coal from the cellar to the kitchen ovens on the fourth floor, when tragedy struck. Machinery from the hotel laundry was put into the lift to be taken downstairs, and as this was taking place, a porter named Daley turned up saying he wanted to ride the lift down, even though it was carrying the heavy machinery. Billy McMullen asked if he could ride the lift down as well, but an engineer named Duff told him he could not, as it would overload the lift, but McMullen jumped in the lift anyway, and refused to get out. The porters then asked if they could operate the lift brake, to which Duff replied that they certainly could not, but one of them chose to disobey him, with tragic consequences! The lift plummeted sixty feet with Duff clinging desperately on to the ropes. One of the heavy iron cog wheels at the top of the shaft was damaged by the lift's sudden descent and heavy load, and it plummeted down the shaft, smashing McMullen's head in. He died instantly. There was a coroner's inquest and the jury returned a verdict of 'accidental death'.

Not long afterwards, the ghost of poor Billy McMullen was seen by many members of staff at the hotel, as well as several guests. A chef had the eerie feeling of being watched one evening, and when he turned to look, he saw the solid-looking ghost of the deceased junior porter, standing in a shadowy corner of the kitchen, gazing at him with a blank expression. The apparition's hair was slicked with blood.

The chef fled from the kitchen, and refused to return until his workplace had been blessed by a priest. The Compton Hotel's owner, Mr Russell, consented to the chef's wishes, and brought in a Catholic priest to bless the kitchen. The blessing was carried out in strict secrecy, so as not to alarm any of the staff outside the kitchen, and it seemed to do the trick - at least for a short while. But then, a fortnight later, McMullen's ghost appeared to Mr Russell himself, materialising at the foot of his bed. When Russell asked, "Is that you, Billy?" the phantom melted away into the darkness.

A tall figure that looks almost as if it is made only from dark vapour has also been seen in the basement of the store, and appears to be rather harmless. The smell of burning sometimes accompanies this apparition, which makes me wonder if it is the ghost of Thomas Henry Sweeting, the youth I told you about earlier, as he was also described as being rather tall.

***

On the opposite side of Church Street, we come to Coopers Buildings where newsagent and bookseller WH Smith was located before it moved around the corner to the new Liverpool One complex. The rooms above WH Smith were haunted by two ghosts, one male the other female, and from all accounts, these apparitions are still occasionally seen in Coopers Buildings, but the identity of the spectres is unknown.

In the 1980s an employee of WH Smiths was singing to herself in a store room at the back of the shop, when she suddenly realised that a female voice was singing along with her, in harmony. When she stopped singing, so did the eerie voice. As soon as she was sure that one of her workmates was not playing a prank on her, she reached for the door handle, ready to flee from the room, and as she did so, she heard a faint chuckling nearby.

Opposite the Cooper Buildings there are two other haunted shops. For many years, a presence has been reported in the basement of a certain greeting card shop on that side of Church Street, and those who have sensed the invisible company of the ghost get the overwhelming feeling it is male. Sometimes the air in the basement becomes suffused with an atmosphere of intense, almost palpable, fear, and some sensitive people have been known to run out of the place in terror.

On that same side of the thoroughfare, there is a clothes shop that stands on the site of the old Henderson Store, which was the scene of a tragic blaze in which eleven people died on Wednesday, 22 June 1960. In the upper floors of the modern shop which occupies this space, strange shadowy figures have been seen and voices heard by security guards, and even phantom aromas of acrid smoke have been reported.

Parker Street, which branches off from Church Street to Clayton Square, also has its fair share of ghosts, and has been the scene of some strange goings-on over the years.

In February 1830, a tobacconist, a confectioners and several other shops on Parker Street were 'robbed' by burglars who could enter and leave the premises without breaking in, or being seen by anyone, even on evenings when the street was being patrolled by a night-watchman. They would then make off with a sizeable quantity of the shops' produce each evening. So exactly who was raiding those three shops? The answer turned out to be most surprising - it was a pack of rats who demonstrated above-average intelligence and cunning.

The rats would begin their nightly raid in the tobacconists, where they nibbled minute holes in the sealskin pouches containing tobacco and after teasing out some of the tobacco leaves, they would carefully transport them back to their nests. In the confectioners, one large rat had gorged itself to such an extent that it was found lying on its back, with its four claws clinging to a type of fairy cake. Another rat then came to its rescue and pulled his fellow rodent by the tail through a small hole in the skirting board, which had been gnawed to a specific diameter to give access to the nest. In the end, this incident, quickly followed by another in which a stick of liquorice - called 'Spanish juice' in those days - was found protruding from a hole in the floor of one of the shops, provided the clues as to the real identity of the mysterious nocturnal thieves. Poison was put down but the rats proved far too clever to fall for that. However, it must have acted as some kind of warning, as the thieving stopped but no dead rodents were ever found. The rat pack seemed to have simply moved on to plague some other area. If you walk into Parker Street from Church Street, take a look at the first building on your right. The upper parts of this building, which dates from 1880, are beautifully designed, with bow windows and ornate carvings. An ashen-faced female head was regularly seen peering out of the top window on the right, up until the 1990s. Just whose ghost it was peering out of that window, and who or what she was hoping to see, remain a mystery, but I do know a person who laid in wait for that ghost many years ago with a telephoto-lensed camera, and he reported that the face was pretty but that the eyes were coal-black and utterly lifeless. The patient ghost-hunter tried to take a picture of what he saw but only captured a blur.

On that same side of Parker Street, there was once a colourful clothing store called Sexy Rexy's, where, around 1981, seventeen-year-old Becky bought a denim shirt as a birthday gift for her brother. As she was paying for the item, she became aware of a young man in his early twenties, staring at her from outside the shop. He wore an off-white jacket with light brown corduroys. He was blond, and Becky thought he bore a resemblance to Martin Fry, lead singer of the band ABC, which was enjoying popularity at that time.

Becky left the shop and made her way to Lewis's, and the blond young man followed her every step of the way, always at a distance, and never attempting to talk to her, or approach her in any way. He stalked her like this, as she made her way through the different departments in Lewis's, and she became so unnerved by his presence that she could not concentrate on her shopping. Eventually, she gave up and hurried out of the store and across Renshaw Street to the bus stop, hoping to catch the next bus to her home on Bagot Street, off Smithdown Road. As luck would have it, the bus arrived very quickly, and Becky was only too glad to get on it and away from the weird stalker. She went upstairs and looked out of the window. There he was, still standing outside one of the Lewis's doorways, his eyes still fixed on her.

About two months after that Becky went to Sexy Rexy's store again, this time to buy her dad a pair of jeans for Father's Day. To her utter amazement, the

Martin Fry look-alike appeared again outside the shop. On this occasion, it was a bright sunny afternoon, and Becky felt confident enough to confront him, but he turned around at her approach and seemed to literally melt away into the milling crowds before she could challenge him.

A week later, on a Saturday morning, Becky was with her mother in the C&A store in Church Street, and who should she see but the same man she had seen on the previous two occasions outside Sexy Rexy's. She was immediately struck by the fact that he was wearing exactly the same clothes - the same off-white jacket and light brown corduroy trousers. She tried to point him out to her mother, but she was too engrossed in hunting down a bargain to pay much attention. The blond-haired stalker circled Becky with his eyes trained on her continuously and then once again seemed to vanish into the crowds of weekend shoppers.

Several weeks went by, during which time Becky had no real reason to go into town, and the stalkings were enough to put her off going in just to browse the shops. However, one day her father asked her to go in with him to do a bit of shopping. She felt safe with him and so she agreed. However, Becky's dad, like most men, soon tired of shopping and went to have a chat with one of his old friends who had a stall at the market that once existed on Church Street. After listening to the two men nattering together for about ten minutes, Becky became bored. "How long are you going to be, Dad?" she asked.

"Sorry, love. We haven't seen each other for ages. We've got a lot of catching up to do."

"Okay, I'll just go and have a look in Owen Owen's

then," said Becky, seeing that it was pointless to argue. "I'll see you in a bit."

As she was making her way towards Owen Owen, on Clayton Square, Becky almost bumped into the blond man, who suddenly appeared out of nowhere, and she jumped back away from him, startled. Seeing him close up, his blue eyes seemed to be encircled with a strange watery redness, almost like liquid blood. The stranger backed away, in the direction of Church Street, and Becky just stood there mute, watching him, transfixed by those strange red-rimmed eyes. She felt ill.

"Hey, lass!" cried a rough voice behind Becky.

She turned, startled, to see a scruffily-dressed beggar in a parka, wearing a greasy pair of faded jeans and dirty badly scuffed trainers. On the ground next to the beggar was a small cardboard box containing a smattering of pennies and ten pence pieces.

"Can you see him?" he asked, nodding his bearded face in the direction of Church Street.

"What?" Becky asked, and then looked back towards Church Street, but the man with the blood-rimmed eyes had now gone.

"That fellah ... Goldilocks ... him you just saw..." continued the beggar, who was suddenly wracked with a chesty cough.

"What about him?"

"He's a bleeding ghost!" exclaimed the vagrant cheerfully and then thanked a passerby for the few shillings she had just dropped in his box.

He told Becky that the man she had a knack of bumping into was actually dead. He had suffered some kind of brain haemorrhage outside Sexy Rexy's store about a year back, and not long afterwards, he had started hanging around the place of his death. "I see a lot of them," continued the beggar, chillingly. "They get confused sometimes and can't accept that they're just spirits, you see." Then he added something that turned Becky's blood to ice on that warm sunny day. "He likes you especially, because you can see him ... most people can't."

Becky did not stop to hear any more, and ran straight back to her dad and told him she was going home. She would not say why, because she knew he would think her crazy, but she implored him to go home with her. He protested, saying he still had things to get in town and he got quite irritated with her, after asking her repeatedly what the matter was, and eventually just told her to "behave".

In the end, Becky lost patience with her dad and ran off to Renshaw Street, where she caught the bus home. She happened to glance back as her bus travelled up Renshaw Street, and suddenly noticed the familiar figure standing outside Lewis's. No doubt about it - it was him - and this time he was waving to her! As the bus drew away, she watched him slowly fade away into nothingness.

Taking into account what the beggar had told her, Becky experienced mixed feelings of fear and sympathy for the troubled ghost. Nevertheless, she had no desire to get involved with a ghost and avoided the city centre for a long time afterwards. When she did eventually pluck up the courage to return to Church Street, she was very edgy, but to date she has not had another encounter with her admirer from beyond.

The old Owen Owen building, which now houses a Tesco Metro, has also acquired a supernatural reputation. The store opened in 1925, in a building that was originally intended to be a hotel, but instead, Owen Owen took it over and it became one of their most famous stores.

A woman who wishes to remain anonymous, who worked at Owen Owen in the 1970s, once encountered a tall distinguished-looking gentleman, in typical Victorian attire, as she worked in an upstairs room. He wore a high white collar, a waistcoat, frock-coat and long striped trousers. When this outdated man came to the witness's attention, he was examining his fob watch. She gasped in surprise and he raised his heavy-lidded eyes from the pocket watch and squinted at her in a very haughty fashion.

The witness ran out of the room to fetch another woman who worked in the store. They both returned to the haunted room and peeped inside. The man was still there, looking out of a window, with his back turned away from them. The women tip-toed away to inform yet another employee about the supernatural visitor, but when he accompanied the women back to the room, the figure was nowhere to be seen, but a very powerful sweet smell was evident - an unusual smell that none of them had ever smelt before and which they could not explain.

On another occasion in the Owen Owen store, a young man serving in one of the departments both saw and felt a hand rest on his left shoulder, but when he turned round, that hand had no arm or body attached. The customer he was serving also saw the hand, and watched as it slowly slid off the young man's shoulder and then vanished.

A woman with mediumistic powers once visited the Owen Owen store after it had closed, and claimed there were at least seven spirits from different eras at large there. They had formed something of a ghostly family over the years. According to the psychic, one of the characters was an old barber, and another was a clerk of some sort, but there were also two women, one of whom, it seemed, had met a violent death at the store a long time ago.

A security guard who later worked at the building when it was being refurbished prior to occupation by another firm, soon discovered the place was haunted when he did his rounds. On one occasion he found an odd-looking pair of antiquated scissors lying on the floor and when he examined them they looked quite blackened, as if they had not been touched for years. The guard put them in his rucksack, but the next morning when he reached home, the scissors were nowhere to be found.

Then the guard and a few of his workmates used a ouija board (in the form of an upturned glass and cut-out letters) at the haunted building one night, and an apparently nonsensical word came through - GORSUCH. The guards laughed at the word and said it proved that the ouija was a load of rubbish. They did not know that in the nineteenth century, a well-known and respected barber named John Gorsuch had his premises on Parker Street. Of course, that would have made some sense of the discovery of the strange scissors.

In the 1880s there was a millinery shop run by a Mademoiselle De Moysey at the location where the health and beauty store Superdrug now stands. There was a suicide at the shop around 1883, when a jilted youth overdosed on laudanum. When the lad was discovered, close to death, the management were less concerned about his welfare, than about the reputation of the shop. So as not to inconvenience the clientele, or bring the wrong sort of attention to the shop, his body was smuggled out before they opened for business, in a canvas bag, and unceremoniously dumped at the hospital on Pembroke Place. Had he received the urgent medical attention that he so obviously required, the young man might have been saved, but instead he was left there to die. Years later, in the 1930s, a dance school moved into rooms over the shop where Superdrug is today. In the 1990s, there were many reports of ghostly silhouettes seen in the windows of the building where the dance school used to be. A shopkeeper who viewed the interior of the building one afternoon with a friend, saw a man and woman dancing together in one of the dusty old rooms. The man had oily slicked back hair and wore a black hammer-tailed tuxedo-styled jacket and black trousers. The woman had a short bob of blonde hair and wore a knee-length pink dress of velvet and chiffon. The shopkeeper called his friend over to the doorway and pointed out the young dancing couple. Seconds later, they had danced away into thin air.

SKELETON CREW

I am sure that some amateur Sherlock Holmes out there will formulate a plausible theory regarding the following unsolved mystery of the sea that has a strong local connection. It unfolded just a few months before the *Mary Celeste* conundrum hit the headlines, but turned out to be much more gruesome than that enigma. Here are the facts of the case.

On the morning of 19 September 1872, the schooner *Lancaster* - on its way from Sydney to New York - was ploughing its way across the Atlantic, when the second mate spotted what seemed to be an abandoned ship adrift off the starboard quarter. He immediately informed the captain, Mr Martin, and by one o'clock, when the heavy winds had subsided, the eerily quiet, weather-beaten ship was drifting alongside the *Lancaster*. Captain Martin, First Mate Rutledge and Second Mate Dugan were lowered down in a rowing a boat and made their way over to the derelict vessel. Once on board, they came upon a truly grotesque scene.

The faded name painted on the dead ship's bowsprit was *Glenalyon*. On deck, below a heap of gale-torn rigging gear and splintered spars, there lay a crushed skeleton in tattered, salt-encrusted clothing. The three men from the *Lancaster* found five further skeletons on the stricken vessel. In the forecastle, a stomach-churning stench of decomposition assailed their nostrils. The skeletal remains of a man lay on a bunk there and two more lay on the floor, each in its own pool of putresence.

With considerable trepidation, the three investigators then visited the captain's cabin, where they were forced to wade, ankle deep, through fetid water, in order to survey the nightmarish scene. The chronometer had stopped at exactly half-past four, and on the captain's table there lay an open Bible (turned downwards), next to a revolver with two chambers loaded. Lying alongside the gun was a sealed bottle containing a message which read, 'Jesus guide this to some helper. Merciful God do not let us perish.'

Some writing and figures on a slate which was used as the ship's temporary log were so blurred as to be illegible, and provided Captain Martin with no clues as to the vessel's last geographical position before some unknown catastrophe struck. The captain's rotting corpse lay on the floor, and nearby on his bed there were books and papers scattered everywhere. One sheet read:

Martinique, May 30th, 1872

Dear Kate,

I will post this letter here, to assure you of my well-being; but do not attempt to hazard an answer to this port, as you will not find me here a week hence. I have kept all my strong promises to you, in spite of a thousand bad advices from my comrades. I drink a little beer but that is all. Your precious photograph is a little silent angel - at least I think it so, and I read your letters over a hundred and a hundred times again. You say in yours, dated from 16 Hope Street Liverpool, that the old man was altogether turned in my favour when he heard of my having passed the Board. Now mind, and keep him so until I get home again, when everything will be comfortable and jolly. Write to Hal's address in St. John, New Brunswick, for should it not reach me there, Hal, at least, will know where I am. Wishing you good health and cheerfulness and good fortune, my own darling Kate,

I am forever your own Robert.

The letter was signed 'Robert C. Hart'. Outside that ill-fated ship, the massive swells through which they had battled in the previous few hours had now gone. The wind had dropped to almost nothing and the sea was now dead calm. A deathly stillness hung over everything like a pall, a stillness in which nothing could be heard but the tiny creaks and moans of the stricken ship.

Captain Martin and his men returned to the *Lancaster* to fetch canvas bags, in order to bury what remained of the *Glenalyon's* captain and crew at sea - an unenviable task, but one which they felt it was their duty, as fellow sailors, to perform. The burials took place that night by the light of the moon and a few oil lamps fastened to the rigging. As the dignified little ceremony was coming to a close, prayers were said and the coffin bags slid, one by one, into the dark sepulchre of the sea. After each little splash, the sea closed over them and they were gone forever.

The doomed Captain Hart's beloved Kate never came forward to throw any light on the contents of his letter, and the resident of Number 16 Hope Street - a teacher of science, English and mathematics named Mr Wilson - remained suspiciously quiet. Was it a plague that left that ship with a 'skeleton crew', or were there more sinister forces at work? Like many a maritime mystery, only the sea itself holds the answer.

HEADLINES IN ADVANCE

On the afternoon of Friday, 17 July 1965, sixteen-year-old Mary Murphy alighted from the Manchester train at Lime Street Station and walked along the platform with her older sister Joyce. As the girls passed a newspaper seller, her attention was caught by the dramatic headline scrawled on his placard: 'AIR CRASH AT SPEKE'.

As Mary lived in Speke, she was naturally alarmed by the headline, but before she could even think about grabbing a copy of the *Liverpool Echo* from the newspaper vendor, Joyce pushed her toward the station exit and pointed to their father, who was standing by his 1962 Tornado Talisman, chatting with a policeman. Believe it or not, Mr Murphy had just had two pints of mild at a pub close to the station, and even if the policeman had smelt Mr Murphy's alcoholic breath, he would not have batted an eyelid, because drink-driving was not recognised as a highly dangerous pastime back in 1965.

Mary and Joyce hurried towards their father, who said, "Come on, Pinky and Perky," - his pet name for his two daughters, after two puppets (of pigs) that were popular with children and adults alike on television in those days. He said goodbye to the policeman, and after Mary claimed the front passenger seat and Joyce sulkily settled in the rear seat, Mr Murphy drove off to join the mighty stream of never-ending traffic on their way home to Speke. During the homeward journey, Mary asked her father if a plane had just crashed in Speke, and he shook his head and said, "Not that I know of, why?"

Mary told him about the headline on the newspaper seller's placard, but Joyce claimed that she had not seen any such headline. Three days later, in the early evening of Tuesday, 20 July, Joyce and Mary sat down in front of the television to watch *Petticoat Junction*, a spin-off comedy from *The Beverley Hillbillies*. The programme started at 6.05pm on Granada, and the Murphy girls loved the show.

At around 6.17pm, a loud explosion shook the Murphy household, quickly followed by distant screams. Within minutes, they were all on the street outside, watching the ominous black mushroom cloud rising up in the distance. A Cambrian Airways' Vickers Viscount plane had crashed into a mothball-making factory - the Mothaks plant. Two women working overtime at this plant were killed, along with the two-man aircrew of the plane, which had overshot the runway at Speke Airport.

Mary Murphy shuddered when she recalled the newspaper headline she had seen on the previous Friday about the 'air crash' at Speke. Had this been a premonition, or a slip in time, which had allowed the teenager to glimpse the next week's news in advance?

There were many reported premonitions of the Mothaks crash, and a Speke woman - Mrs James - told her doctor, husband and neighbours that she had been having super realistic nightmares about a plane crashing close to her house. The doctor said the nightmares were merely caused by anxiety; perhaps a subconscious fear of a plane crashing into her home, because of its proximity to the airport.

I once experienced the phenomenon of 'headlines in advance' myself, and found it as unsettling as it was baffling. On Thursday, 13 March 2008, I was shopping in a supermarket when I overheard someone talking about Arthur C Clarke's death. Being an avid science-fiction reader in my youth, I was dismayed to hear of the author's death. At home I checked the news, and was surprised to find that there was no mention of his death, nor was there a word of the modern prophet's demise on the Internet.

Six days later, Arthur C Clarke passed away, on 19 March 2008, in Sri Lanka. I was stunned, especially as something similar had happened to me once before. On 6 March 2003, I was appearing on the Billy Butler Show, on Radio Merseyside, talking about the paranormal. Alec Young was taking calls from listeners who all had stories for me. A caller who referred to himself as "Ken from Southport", told Alec that the singer and actor Adam Faith had just died. Alec mentioned this to Billy and me, and the radio station's news team were consulted, but when they checked, Adam Faith was apparently still alive and kicking. Billy Butler checked Ceefax just to be sure, and confirmed that there was no news of Adam Faith's death.

Then, on Saturday, 8 March, Adam Faith did die of a heart attack, aged just sixty-two. Billy Butler said it was like something out of *The Twilight Zone*, and he urged Ken of Southport to phone back, but he never did, and his number could not be traced.

HOTEL IN ANOTHER DIMENSION

Not all timewarps are the result of some random, poorly understood but natural phenomenon. From my long-term study of the subject, it seems that, on occasion, something is bringing the past back into the present, often for sinister reasons, and this something has an intelligence.

For decades, a fuzzy dark humanoid shape has regularly manifested itself inside the Adelphi Hotel on Lime Street, and whenever it is at large, a sequence of inexplicable events take place. I first heard about this entity in the 1980s, but it dates back to at least 1970, the year of the earliest report.

In August 1970, Simon, a London businessman with the unusual surname of Wellbeloved, was about to leave the Adelphi to visit a friend's shop on Hanover Street, when the receptionist told him he was wanted urgently on the telephone. Simon took the receiver from the receptionist and listened to a distraught female voice at the other end of the line. It was his ex-wife Barbara, and she told him that she was deeply depressed and could not bear life without him. She sounded as if she had been drinking, and threatened to take an overdose of sleeping pills if he did not come back to her. Simon eventually managed to calm her down somewhat and talk her out of her suicide bid. She apologised for being a nuisance before hanging up.

Simon felt so upset by the call that he decided to go back up to his room and not visit his friend after all. Lost in thought, he took the elevator, rather than the stairs. Sharing it with him was a young woman, probably in her twenties. An eerie sound enveloped the elevator as it made its way up the shaft - a sound like a howling gale. The woman turned anxiously towards Simon, hoping that he had an innocent explanation for the roaring sound, but he was equally bewildered and became even more alarmed when the elevator began to rock slightly from side to side. Faint, unintelligible voices could be heard in the wailing current of air, and then the elevator came to an abrupt halt on its upward journey.

The young woman looked about in panic, and rushed futilely from one side of the lift to the other, but she stopped dead and fell silent when the dark grey outline of a man, consisting only of swirling vapours, slowly emerged from out of the elevator wall, and stood there, apparently trying to solidify into a man with a white shirt, dark waistcoat and black shiny shoes. The clothes and shoes seemed solid enough for about five seconds or so, but the head remained vapourous. The eyes were two dark rounded holes, and the mouth was a slit of blackness. The nose and ears were non-existent, but the forehead and hair kept going in and out of focus. The young woman lost all inhibition and grabbed hold of Simon's shirt and hid behind his back, trembling, but the businessman stood his ground and stared in disbelief at the apparition. The two voices they had heard became more distinct, and were definitely those of a man and a woman, but strangely they both seemed to be emanating from this 'thing'. About twenty seconds after it had emerged through the elevator wall, the thing returned the way it had come. The whistling wind sound stopped immediately, and the elevator continued smoothly on its way. When it reached the next floor, Simon and the woman got out at once, immensely relieved to be on solid ground again. She was so spooked by the encounter that she checked out of the Adelphi that evening and found alternative accommodation in a hotel on Mount Pleasant.

More inexplicable things happened to Simon after the episode in the elevator. On the following morning he was sitting in the hotel lounge, sipping a cup of coffee as he perused a copy of *The Times*, when an article entitled, 'Mr Kennedy's Setback' took his interest, and he began to read it. The gist of the article was that the House of Representatives had refused to give President Kennedy long-term borrowing authority for increased foreign aid.

The reference to a president who had been dead since his assassination in 1963, immediately struck Simon as unreal. America's current president was Richard Nixon, so how could a responsible staid newspaper such as *The Times* print such a howler?

Then Simon scanned the rest of the broadsheet, and was amazed to discover that it was dated August 1961. He took the crisp, new-looking but apparently outdated copy of *The Times* over to the receptionist, to see if it had been put there deliberately. She had to agree that the newspaper was indeed seven years out of date, but was at a loss to explain how it had come to be there, so she simply shrugged and smiled.

Simon took the backdated newspaper to his friend Roy at the shop on Hanover Street, but when he looked at the newspaper, he could find nothing amiss. There was a somewhat controversial portrait of Princess Margaret on the front page, and inside the newspaper, articles about seabed dumping of industrial waste, Tony Jacklin the golfer, and other rather mundane news - but definitely no mention of President Kennedy. Simon then checked the date on the newspaper - 21 August 1970. Inexplicably the date, together with the newspaper's content, had somehow reverted to normal.

When Simon returned to the Adelphi, he sat in the lounge for a while, trying to take stock of the bizarre events of the last twenty-four hours, but he could not come up with any rational explanation for them. Simon was a wood-pulp agent, and at 2pm that afternoon he drove up to a timber firm near Blackburn, where he brokered a very lucrative deal. At 7pm, he was back at the Adelphi for the last time, and over a drink at the hotel bar, he got talking to a retired brigadier who was staying in the city for a week. This widower was not only surprisingly knowledgeable about business and economics, to say that he had spent his working life in the army, but he also had an interest in what was then termed the supernatural, and he astounded Simon by mentioning the weird activity that periodically took place at the hotel.

For the past seven years, every August, he had stayed at the hotel, even though his married children (all living in the suburbs of Liverpool) had repeatedly invited him to stay with them. On each occasion, without fail, the brigadier had witnessed some kind of inexplicable phenomena at the hotel. He too had witnessed the vortex of wind when using the elevator and had also seen the materialisation of the ghostly man. The staff had become rather used to guests forever enquiring about strange noises and shadows in the elevator, and of peculiar slips in time.

"What sort of slips in time?" asked Simon, mindful of the newspaper that had inexplicably displayed the printed news of almost ten years ago. The brigadier said that certain parts of the hotel's interior had a habit of changing back to the way they were in the 1930s, the 1950s, or the 1960s. The old military man had made enquiries amongst the staff about the strange goings-on, and had gleaned the following information about one particular event.

Raymond Frank Brown, a fifteen-year-old pageboy, had tragically died after becoming trapped in the baggage room lift of hotel, in August 1961. Raymond, of Walton's Salop Street, had only been working at the Adelphi for a fortnight, but during that time he had established himself as a well-liked and conscientious young man, who got on well with the rest of the hotel staff.

On the night of Monday, 21 August 1961, the teenager was taken down to the hotel basement in the baggage room lift by another pageboy, fifteen-year-old John Whittaker. It was Raymond's intention to fetch some coffee from the basement storeroom in order to make a drink for the hotel's night doorman, Patrick Curley. John left him in the basement and returned to the upper floors, and minutes later he learned, to his horror, that Raymond had become trapped in the lift.

The doorman, Curley, heard an agonised cry from the basement and ran down to discover that Raymond was trapped between the lift platform and the underside of the ground floor. It was thought he had been trying to climb into the lift after he had started it. Pageboys were not authorised to use that lift and a warning sign inside it stated that fact very plainly, although they sometimes failed to heed it, if no one was looking.

Firemen were soon at the scene, and they cut through a safety bar to free Raymond, who, by that time, had lapsed into unconsciousness, and they gently wrapped him in a blanket. He was taken to the Royal Hospital on Pembroke Place, but was pronounced dead on arrival. He had died from asphyxiation. The coroner recorded a verdict of death by misadventure.

Why had Raymond returned to the lift without the coffee he had gone down to the basement to fetch? That very pertinent question was never answered, and we will probably never know the exact circumstances that led to his death, but for many years afterwards, the ghost of a pageboy was seen in the Adelphi by scores of witnesses - including the brigadier himself.

On one occasion, American tourists staying at the world-famous hotel told the desk clerk they had heard a boy talking in the lift, even though no boy could be seen, and on that same day, a Norwegian guest had just booked into his room when his suitcase rose off the floor - as if lifted by invisible hands - and then crossed the foyer to a staircase. On another occasion a Cheshire woman staying at the Adelphi saw a semi-transparent boy wearing what she described as military attire - or could it just have been a pageboy's uniform?

The brigadier had a theory that something was invading our dimension, and in the process, was bringing the past into the present. Unfortunately, Simon Wellbeloved had to return home to London on the following day, although he visited the Adelphi Hotel on several other occasions in the hope of experiencing more timeslips and ghostly phenomena, but unfortunately he saw and heard nothing out of the ordinary during his other stays at the hotel.

The brigadier became something of a regular guest at the Adelphi until his death in the mid-1970s. Staff and guests have written to me over the years, and all have mentioned the unearthly sensation of bygone times 'seeping' back into the present. One employee heard what sounded like a ragtime band playing in the hotel's Sefton Suite (which, incidentally, is an exact replica of the *Titanic's* smoking lounge) at four o'clock in the morning. As soon as he opened the doors to the spacious room, the music stopped dead, but the staff member had an intense feeling of being watched from the darkness within the suite. That same week, another member of staff heard the midnight chimes of a clock in the foyer - but this timepiece could not be located, despite an exhaustive search.

One night in the 1960s, two policemen rushed into the foyer, claiming that a man was threatening to jump out of a second floor window on the Brownlow Hill side of the hotel. It turned out that the room in question was unoccupied that night, but the police were told about a man with slicked back hair and a toothbrush moustache who had jumped to his death from that window decades before. The man the police had seen sitting on the second storey window ledge had worn a black hammer tail coat, and had slicked back hair and a black 'Hitler' moustache. When the policemen returned to Brownlow Hill, the man was gone from the window ledge, but the window was seen to open, apparently all by itself.

The Edwardian Adelphi has undergone extensive refurbishment in recent years, but the past of that glorious building continues to spill over into the more mediocre present-day era. Although the elevator in which Raymond Brown had his fatal accident has now been relocated, the vortex, and its whispering voices, is still experienced today.

Inger, a tourist who has travelled the world, has a penchant for Liverpool, and in April 2000, she, her boyfriend Ilya, and friend Jenni visited the Adelphi. They went out for dinner on the first day of their stay, and then returned to the hotel. Around midnight the trio decided to sample the famous Liverpool nightlife and agreed to give the American Bar downstairs a try.

They entered the hotel elevator and Ilya pressed the ground floor button. The doors closed but the lift failed to descend. No movement was felt, so Inger stabbed the ground floor button with her finger, after which the lift plummeted, seeming to go into free-fall. The often-reported wind was heard to howl around the elevator, accompanied by the male and female voices talking simultaneously. The elevator eventually decelerated and came to a halt on the ground floor, and the three visitors stepped out unsteadily on to the plush carpet of the lobby, each of them lost for words.

There are four hundred and two rooms in the Adelphi, and each room has a tale to tell. A whole book could be written on the supernatural goings-on at the place, but I am of the opinion that time is the real culprit in a majority of these cases, and not earthbound spirits.

In one room, in 2006, a female guest awoke to find a woman in black standing in the full-length mirror of her wardrobe. Her face was buried in her hands and she was obviously sobbing, but not a single sound came from her. The ghost had her hair tied up in a bun and wore an intricate white lace collar. Even curiouser, the room glimpsed behind the spectre in the mirror was not a reflection of the modern hotel room, but a blue wallpapered room, dimly lit by a gas jet over a mantelpiece. As soon as the hotel guest flipped open her mobile, with the intention of calling her mother to tell her about the ghost, the woman in the mirror vanished, along with the reflection of the quaint old-fashioned room.

Many years ago, in the old Adelphi hotel - which stood on the site of the present day one (which was built in 1912), there was a report of a buzzing sound, which gradually increased in volume and disturbed the quiet calm of the hotel lounge one evening. As the noise rose to an unbearable pitch, several people reported an all-enveloping darkness, which filled the lounge and blotted out the light from the chandeliers. In the end, some guests and members of staff could not even see their hands in front of their faces.

Minutes later the weird localised darkness faded away as mysteriously as it had arrived.

I wonder if there are beings in a parallel dimension that try to get through to our dimension of time, perhaps out of curiosity, or perhaps motivated by plain mischief. These beings might be responsible for the timeslips at the hotel, and also for some inexplicable disappearances and reappearances of various objects. For example, in 1977, a man named Robert Hault was ready to go to bed at a room in the Adelphi one night, when seconds after he turned off the light, something fell on to his bed with a gentle thud. Robert quickly switched the light back on to find a copy of Moriarty's Police Law lying on the bed; a book of practical legal knowledge that was known to generations of policemen as the 'Copper's Bible'.

This edition, which had literally fallen out of thin air on to Robert Hault's bed, was a 1964 seventeenth edition hardback. Inside the book, on a blank page, someone had written the name James Jones in pencil. Hault decided to keep the book, and years later he showed it to me, after hearing me talking about ghostly goings-on in the Adelphi on the radio.

I mentioned the incident of the falling book whilst on air, and a James Jones came forward to tell me how, in 1966, he had been staying at the Adelphi, and had lost his seventeenth edition of *Moriarty's Police Law*. That year, Mr Jones had been a budding police cadet, but illness later prevented him from joining the force. Mr Jones was also able to describe two bookmarks that were found in that book - something I had not mentioned on air - they were cigarette cards featuring cricketers.

Mr Jones recalled how, in 1966, he had been reading that book whilst lying on his bed, and had put it down for a moment whilst he went to stretch his legs and look out of the window for a few moments. In those few seconds the law book vanished without trace, even though there was no one else in the room. He searched everywhere for it, but to no avail. Something had evidently taken that book whilst his back was turned and returned it, still in its pristine condition, in the same hotel room eleven years later.

THE NAKED LADY OF ISLINGTON

Daylight dwindles and the hours of darkness increase, until those with a nine to five job never see their house in daylight from one weekend to the next - welcome to winter. In my long years of ghost-hunting, winter has always been a period of unusually high supernatural activity. Why should this be so? Well, long before the current Gregorian calendar of twelve uneven months was introduced, there was a thirteen-month calendar of three hundred and sixty-four days, based on the Moon, which was used well into Tudor times.

Before that time there existed other calendars, such as the Celtic one, and even further back there was Mindris, a lost calendar based on Mother Nature herself - the planet Earth - which was envisaged as a living female being (nowadays known as Gaia), whose harmonic energies waxed and waned, thereby causing the seasons. In this ancient reckoning, our January lies in Missel, a period associated with darkness and the unquiet dead, spanning the period between Halloween and Valentine's Day. However, all calendars agree on one thing: winter is the season of dusk, of night mists, of spirits, be it by sputtering tallow candle, or neon light. Many years ago, in the 1920s, an elderly widow by the name of Catherine Jones, lived on St Anne Street, Everton. She dreaded the month of January, but not because she suffered from Sad Syndrome (Sad standing for Seasonally-Affected Depression), or yearned for the blue skies of summer, but for something much more sinister. After dark in that wintry month, a strange apparition was seen and heard in the immediate vicinity of her home - a naked lady, wearing nothing but a wedding ring. The ghost seemed to come from the direction of Clare Street, usually at around midnight, and was seen by patrolling policemen, night watchmen and a number of other people who worked late.

Many people in an area bounded by Christian Street, the Islington High Street and St Anne Street, saw the nude phantom walking along singing that old Victorian song 'Annie Laurie' in a most melancholy voice. When anyone approached the ghost, she would instantly fade away into the night, like the dying chimes of a midnight clock. Catherine Jones was a woman with psychic powers, and to her, the ghost looked very solid indeed. Some saw the entity as a nebulous blur of light, like a moving will-o'-the-wisp, whereas others saw it as a solid carnate person, apparently as real as you or me.

One snowy January night, in 1921, at around 11.30pm, Catherine Jones and her eldest daughter

Mary were walking home from the house of a former neighbour, Mrs Murray. Mrs Murray's daughter had given birth to a baby boy at her mother's house a few hours earlier, and Catherine and Mary had been present at the birth and had joined in the toast to the newborn child's health.

As Mrs Jones and her daughter carefully trod their way over an icy mantle of frozen snow on Islington Street, they could see that Christian Street, across the road, was deserted, until they both noticed a figure approaching in the distance, barely visible by the feeble glow-worm lamps. At first, the figure seemed to be wearing light clothes, or so they thought, for when mother and daughter reached the junction of Springfield Street, the two of them could plainly see that they were looking at a naked woman, and she was walking barefoot on the ice-crusted pavements straight towards them.

Mary panicked, and attempted to pull her mother across the road to the other side of Christian Street, but instead, she sent her off balance and the fifty-year-old woman fell with a heavy thud on to her back. Seconds later, Mary slipped and fell on to her right knee, scraping a hole in her dress. The naked woman was now just twenty feet away from them and Catherine lay gasping for air, as the fall had badly winded her, and her faint breath was visible as a grey vapourous exhalation. Mary's breath came in short heavy bursts, as she panted with fear at the approach of the ghostly woman. Her exhalations were visible as staccato plumes of mist - but the ghost had no visible exhaled breath, and she began to sing:

Her brow is like the snow drift,
Her neck is like the swan,
Her face is the fairest
That ever the sun shone on...

Mary let out a scream, which triggered the instant dematerialisation of the unclothed woman. Catherine and Mary slipped three more times as they scrambled across an iced over puddle in the cobbled road. A cartwheel had passed over the frozen puddle earlier, giving it the appearance of smashed glass. The two women were in a terrible state by the time they reached home. With frozen trembling hands, Mary tried to get a fire going in the grate with a lit taper, whilst her mother shuddered speechless in the fireside chair.

They were later somewhat relieved to hear that the ghost had been seen by a few other people that morning, including a policeman and a milk-delivery boy on Clare Street. By the 1950s, as the post-war bulldozers began to alter the north end of the city, the ghost was rarely seen but occasionally heard around Christian Street, singing songs like Mary of Argyll and other old-fashioned ballads. Is there a story behind this unusual haunting? It would seem that there is. I have researched this case and have gleaned the following information.

In January 1899, a prospective female tenant went to view a small dwelling at Number 10 Spring Place, off Springfield Street, close to Christian Street. These dwellings on Spring Place were principally inhabited by working-class people, and Number 10 had lain empty for some time. The keys were obtained from the house next door, and the woman let herself into the dwelling.

On the upper floor of the building she came across a beautiful naked woman, with long raven-black hair, lying on the floor on top of a bundle of old rags. The woman, who looked as if she was in her late twenties, was very obviously dead, yet she wore a serene expression and there were no marks or bruises upon her body to indicate the cause of her death.

In the same room, a pair of women's boots was found, and in an adjoining room, a woman's green jacket and a portion of a chemise. In the room below the one in which the body was discovered, a black straw hat was found. The unknown woman wore a wedding ring, but there were no papers or other articles found within the house, by which identification could be made by the police. A downstairs window was broken and it was discovered that the lock on the door to the house could easily be opened by almost any old key. No one in the immediate neighbourhood knew the naked woman's identity and no one had seen her enter the house. The corpse, which was unusually well-preserved, perhaps because of the freezing winter temperatures, was conjectured to have lain in the house for approximately two weeks.

The postmortem examination yielded no clues as to how the naked woman had died, and although death by starvation was originally assumed to have been the cause of her demise, the coroner discovered that the body was, in fact, perfectly well-nourished. Why had the woman stripped off her clothes and chemise, to (presumably) sleep on top of a few old rags during that freezing weather? Why were some of her clothes found in other rooms? And what had happened to her skirt and underwear?

Mrs Watt, a thirty-year-old street singer, contacted the police and claimed that the naked woman was Anne Smith, a vocalist from Manchester who had fallen on hard times in recent years and had been forced to sing ballads on the streets. Around the same time, a railway porter in Chester claimed the unidentified nude had been his wife, but his claim was never proven. Fifty-three-year-old Joe Lancaster, who owned and ran a women's lodging house at Numbers 121-123 Richmond Row, apparently backed up Mrs Watt's story, and told the police that both the naked woman and Mrs Watt had stayed at his lodging house.

There certainly seems to be more to this case than immediately meets the eye, and one cannot help thinking that perhaps the naked woman met her death at the hands of a killer who was one step ahead of the police. The dead woman wore a wedding ring, yet her husband, if he was alive at the time of the macabre discovery, never came forward. There are one or two other things that nag me about the lodging house in Richmond Row.

In March 1896, Mrs Margaret Starkey, the widowed sister of one Bridget Corfield, put the following notice in the Missing Relatives column of a national newspaper:

News wanted of Bridget Corfield, or any of her relations. Formerly of Hulme, Manchester. Her widowed sister, Margaret Starkey, care of Editor, inquiries.

Someone reading *Reynolds Newspaper*, the broadsheet

that carried the notice, knew that sixty-one-year-old Bridget Corfield was staying at Lancaster's Lodging House, on Richmond Row in Liverpool, and they contacted the editor of the newspaper. The editor, in turn, contacted Starkey, and a sum of money was sent to Bridget, as her sister Margaret had received a large insurance payout after the death of her husband, and wished to share it with her.

Yet Corfield chose to stay at the lodging house, and had no intention of spending the money she had received from her sister on buying a house or apartment for herself. She was a very careful woman, but her weakness was drink. By 1900, Corfield had frittered away almost half of her sister's generous gift, leaving her with around two-hundred pounds - which still, in today's money, would amount to thousands of pounds.

Bridget was still living in Joe Lancaster's lodging house on Richmond Row, and one Sunday evening, in May 1900, a doctor was called to the premises. According to Lancaster, Bridget had tripped and fallen down the lodging house stairs. Her injuries were so severe that the doctor could do nothing more than dab at her swollen head with a cold towel, and Bridget died that night. A verdict of accidental death was later returned and the whereabouts of her money after the accident remained something of a mystery; no one ever found it.

Around the time Bridget died from her 'fall', a man in his mid-fifties by the name of Robert Jones, came to stay at Lancaster's lodging house. He too was rumoured to have a little nest egg, and was a bit eccentric.

In July of that year, Jones was found in a semi-conscious state lying on the pavement in Aubrey Street, Everton. He was taken to Mill Road Infirmary after he managed to tell the police constable who found him that he was lodging in Lancaster's on Richmond Row. Four days later he passed away in hospital, and his money was never found. Could these suspicious deaths somehow tie in with the case of the naked woman whose body was found at Number 10 Spring Place the year before, in 1899? Was Anne Smith - or whatever her real name was - in fact murdered for some sinister reason? Surely it was her restless ghost which haunted Islington for many years - perhaps because she longed for her killer to be brought to justice?

TAKE IT EASY

One damp, blustery evening in the washout summer of 2007, three men, all in their fifties, sat in a corner of the parlour of a quiet little pub in Liverpool city centre. John was a practical, simple man; gravelly voiced, of tall stature, but old before his time, with receding snow-white hair and a weathered leathery face. He bore a slight resemblance to the late hard-boiled actor Lee Marvin.

Then there was Ronnie, a perpetual worrier, whose irritating and often repeated catchphrase was, "Take it easy", even though that was the last thing he was able to do himself. He used that line whenever he thought that John was on the point of punching someone, or saying something offensive. Ronnie also had the annoying habit of repeatedly glancing at his watch whenever you were talking to him, as though he had other, more urgent, matters to attend to.

Phil, the third member of this trio, was from Huyton, but you would never have guessed it from his plummy, accent-less voice. He spoke like a 1930s BBC radio broadcaster, and his manners were equally impeccable. He never swore, used vulgar language, or entered into a heated argument, but his one failing was his encyclopaedic knowledge of, and obsession with, all things medical.

Phil knew bits and pieces of information about every disease, ailment and condition afflicting the human body and mind, without having a true medical understanding of any of them. He often misdiagnosed John and Ronnie's symptoms when they suffered from such innocuous maladies as sore throats, allergies and indigestion. On one occasion, Phil's diagnosis of Ronnie's twitching lower eyelid led to the latter visiting a solicitor to draw up his will, although it turned out to be nothing more serious than a bit of eye strain.

"Could you turn that thing down please?" John shouted through the hatchway, his grey-blue eyes swivelling between the booming television set up on its shelf and the young student working as a bar tender. The barman obligingly reached for the remote control and lowered the volume.

Ronnie shook his head and sighed as he looked at Phil. "Sit down, John, will you? You've got me on edge here," he said to his tetchy friend.

"The worst thing they ever did was ban smoking in these places," John complained, producing a small tin of cheroots from his inside jacket pocket. "What could they do to me if I lit up anyway?"

"They could fine you, for a start," Ronnie told him, and angled his head as he smiled.

"Who could? You mean him in there? That puny student? I'd kill him first." Nevertheless, John suddenly thought better of it and took up his usual place at the little round red-topped table and with a grumble, put the tin of cigars back in his pocket.

"Probably a good thing. Those stogies will kill you if you keep on smoking them," Phil announced. "Have you any idea how many chemicals there are ..."

"Oh! For Pete's sake, shut up, Phil!" said John, dismissively. "You're like an old woman."

Phil, hurt that nobody ever took his medical advice seriously, tilted his head back and sulkily pretended to be studying a cheap framed photograph of St George's Hall on the wall above them.

"I hope there's a war, I do," said John, gripping his pint glass of bitter.

"Don't say that," Ronnie gasped, and looked at Phil to back him up, but he was still looking at the picture in a noncommunicative mood.

"If there was a world war, they'd be chucking cigarettes at us right left and centre," John muttered, and he sat in the padded ersatz leather chair, studying the toll that time had taken on the backs of his hands in the form of ugly liver spots and wrinkles. He gritted his dentures. A few weeks ago, on 1 July, smoking in all enclosed spaces and workplaces had been prohibited in England, and John had a twenty-a-day habit. He detested standing outside in the rain with a soggy ciggie in his mouth on wet nights like this. It made him feel like such a loser.

Just then, a man in his early thirties walked into the pub parlour. His hair was long and straggly, and his face was very pale, because he was wearing thick make-up. Under each eye, on the cheek bone, he sported a black diamond. The stranger's eyes were encircled in thick, panda-style eyeliner that had the consistency and shine of black boot polish. The oddball's funereal overcoat went right down below the knees, and was scuffed, well worn, and covered in nodes of unsightly fuzz.

John made a deliberate point of looking him up and down and swore slowly under his breath. "Oh my God!" he said, in his usual condescending attitude towards Goths, or anybody who was different in any way.

Fortunately, the Goth didn't seem to hear him. He was looking across the room towards the hatchway, but he didn't go and order a drink, but just sat down near the door.

An old woman came into the parlour seconds later and shook her brolly. "It's like a friggin' monsoon out there," she said, addressing no one in particular, then went to the hatchway and ordered a drink. John grinned, because the old woman had accidentally flicked some of the rainwater from her umbrella into the Goth's face, but he acted as if he was not at all bothered and didn't even flinch.

"It was warm today," said Phil, snapping out of his spell of self-pity, "and then next thing it's raining cats and dogs. Changes in the weather like that can kill, you know," he told John and Ronnie. He never seemed to learn his lesson.

Ignoring this latest little gem from his friend, John suddenly reached into his trouser pocket and pulled out his new slimline mobile phone. He took a sip from his drink and then smiled in an uncharacteristically mellow way. "Can either of you remember your first ever phone number?" he asked.

Ronnie looked up, and concentrating hard, said, "First ever telephone we had installed was ... ooh let's see ... way back in nineteen seventy-four."

"That late?" smirked Phil. "We had a one way back in nineteen sixty-eight."

"Our number was 708..." Ronnie struggled to recall the rest of the digits. "That's it!" he said suddenly, nodding slightly with his index finger pointing at the ceiling and then recited the last four digits.

"Can't remember the first number we had, but when we moved to West Derby, in nineteen seventy-seven, it was a 226 number," John remembered, and he pictured his late mother sitting by the telephone table in the hall. Suddenly he was able to reel off the telephone number, just as she used to say it when she was answering a call, and he suddenly felt a deep longing to be back there with his mum.

"Imagine if you could just dial your old number and speak to your mum," said Ronnie, before checking his watch for the umpteenth time that night. For the first time in twenty-odd years, Phil and Ronnie saw John's eyes fill up with unshed tears. It was the nearest the hard man had ever come to showing them that he was as vulnerable as they were under his hard shell. "I'm going to phone my old number," John suddenly announced, and he slid his mobile open and began to key in a number he had not dialled for years.

"John! Don't be daft, mate," Ronnie warned him. That's somebody else's number now. You'll be making a nuisance call."

But John took no notice of his friend's advice and carried on dialling. "That's strange ... very strange," he muttered, studying the screen.

"What is?" asked Phil.

"I keyed in 051, instead of the new prefix code 0151, and I've got a ringing tone." John's eyes narrowed as he pressed the mobile hard against his left ear.

"Don't you remember? The area code used to be 051..." Ronnie reminisced, then told John to hang up before someone answered.

Too late - someone had already picked up the phone and a very familiar woman's voice answered and sent John's heart racing.

"Hello?" said John's long-dead mother. There was no mistaking that distinctive voice, which he had tried to replay in his head so many times over the years, whenever he hankered after some memory of the good old days.

"Mum? It's me ... John." John's mouth was drying up. He slowly reached for his pint of bitter as he heard the background sounds on the other end of the line into the past. It was the theme tune to Nationwide, a current affairs television programme his mum used to watch every day after they had finished their tea.

"That's not John ... who is it?" his mother asked, with a voice full of suspicion.

"Mum, it is me," John insisted. He began to feel a severe discomfort in his chest and he broke out in a cold sweat.

She hung up on him.

"I got through!" cried John, looking at Phil and Ronnie, in a state of utter confusion. "I got through! It was my mum! She was there!" He quickly pressed the redial button, but the robotic voiced operator came on the line saying the number had not been recognised. This time John redialled the number of his old home manually, but became very irritated when he again heard the same error message.

"John, your mother passed away twenty years ago," said Phil, softly. He glanced at Ronnie, who also looked concerned.

"Oh, did she? I forgot about that, Phil!" snapped John, through gritted teeth. "I know she's dead, but she just answered a phone call I made to my old house. Alright?"

"She just sounded like your mum, John ... that's all," Ronnie told him, as he looked at his friend's fingers frantically dialling on the mobile again.

"Sorry, the number you have dialled has not been recognised ... Sorry, the number ..." came the tinny voice from the mobile's earpiece. John emitted the C word for everyone present to hear and threw the mobile on to the table and did not dial again. He just sat there shaking his head. "I could hear the music for that programme - Nationwide" he said, "and that's not on the telly nowadays is it? How do you explain that then? Eh? Come on, Ronnie, you've usually got all the answers clever arse."

At this point, Phil rose from his chair. "Er, my round ... the usual?" he asked, trying to diffuse the rising tension.

Ronnie nodded and tried to smile, but his face betrayed the fact that he was worried about John's behaviour.

John, meanwhile, thought he was losing his mind. He looked again at the number he had dialled on the screen of his mobile. It had begun with 051, a now obsolete area code. He was not going to risk ridicule by dialling that number again whilst he was still with his friends, but he fully intended to try it again the minute he got home. Perhaps it was something to do with time; a timeslip allowing him to dial into the past, maybe? It was all extremely baffling. John looked up and saw that the Goth was now looking at him with what he took to be a patronising smile. It really irritated John and he felt the anger boil up inside him. The audacity of the 'freak' - as John regarded the people of that subculture. "Who d'you think you're smiling at, hey? You pasty-faced bastard!"

The Goth's panda eyes widened in surprise. He turned around, as if he thought John must be addressing someone behind him, but there was no one there. He smiled again, and in a well spoken voice, asked, "Can you actually see me?"

John was always suspicious of other people's motives, especially strangers, and he immediately assumed he was 'taking the mickey' and swore at him, which brought the Goth hovering across the room towards his table in one steady smooth movement, as if he were on castors. John recoiled in shock when he realised that the stranger's feet were about five inches above the ground.

"Jesus!" he shrieked, and rocketed up from his chair, catching the table with his knee and sending Ronnie's almost empty glass crashing to the floor. "You can see me!" said the floating figure, full of excitement. His body lurched forward and his chalk-white face was thrust right into John's face. His black lips opened as he laughed. John could not see the joke, but instead of getting angry, he covered his face with his hands.

Ronnie shot to his feet and reached out for John's arm, asking if he was okay. He could not see the Goth at all, it later transpired and nor could Phil. That really did it; now John was convinced that he was going insane. First the call to the 1970s and now he was being persecuted by a man in black with a clown-like face. He rushed into the pub toilet, where he repeatedly dowsed his face with cold water over the wash basin. He looked in the mirror, and as he tried to rationalise the weird things that had been happening, he saw the pale face of the ghost rise up slowly over his right shoulder in the reflection in the glass.

"Get away from me!" he shouted, and backed away towards the door.

"John, John, take it easy," said the eerie phantom, "I put your call through to your mother before. It was me!"

Some of John's fear evaporated when he heard these words, and he stood there intrigued, ready to run out, should the ghost turn nasty.

"Would you like to talk to her again?" asked the Goth, a question which, of course, was very tempting.

John stood there, his heart pounding, with beads of sweat bursting out from his forehead. He suddenly felt nauseous. The ghost promised that he could talk to his mother whenever he wanted, if he was prepared to do just do one simple thing. He then went on to give him some chilling instructions.

The one 'simple' thing turned out to be not quite so simple. John was to go to a certain house and kill an old man named Roland. That man - a former tough biker - had murdered the Goth, back in the 1970s, by hanging him from a noose in the building which had now been converted into the pub which was currently frequented by John and his friends. Today was the thirtieth anniversary of the hanging and he had come back to pay a visit.

John, despite his hard-man reputation, was not prepared to commit murder for anyone, and he turned round and yanked open the toilet door to find Phil and Ronnie coming to find him. He glanced back to see that the ghost had now gone. John's two close friends jumped aside in surprise as he rushed between them and ran out of the pub.

When Phil and Ronnie caught up with him in the next street, they asked him what was going on, and John said he wished he knew. He gave an account of the apparition and what he had proposed, and while Phil predictably advised him to see his doctor, Ronnie believed his friend had genuinely experienced something paranormal, and advised him instead to visit a priest. For once, John took his advice and did just that. He was blessed by the priest and found great solace in his kind words. He also became a regular churchgoer from that time on and he now stays well away from that haunted pub.

I have since discovered that two other people have had encounters with the sinister Goth, in the same local used by the three men. How did the ghost allow John to make a telephone call to his mother in a bygone decade? Perhaps it merely created that illusion in John's mind, drawing upon his memories to fabricate the incident, or, perhaps ghosts really can manipulate radio waves and electrical currents so as to allow telephonic communication with someone in the past. It is known that they certainly can meddle with modern electrical devices. A common antic staged by ghosts is the kettle which turns itself on, or the electric doorbell that rings by itself.

In the 1990s, I talked to a former telecommunications engineer who was called out by a well-known Liverpool business firm to trace the 'joker' who was making daily nuisance telepone calls to three women who worked at the same store. Despite using the latest tracing technology, the caller was never found. The mysterious caller predicted a certain member of staff would die within six months, and, sure enough, three months later the person in question collapsed and died instantly in his office from a heart attack. A medium was even brought in by the manager of the store to see if a ghost was responsible, and something tore off the psychic's toupee as he walked around the upper floors of the store one evening.

After a year of nuisance calls and ghostly goings-on at the store, the caller apparently hung up, hopefully for good. It would seem that ghosts are now becoming rather proficient at controlling all kinds of technology, from computers, to mobile phones and even to iPods. All of these devices use tiny microchips which contain circuits that cannot be seen by the naked eye. There is some evidence that the electrons which these circuits use can be influenced by the power of the mind, and perhaps the ghost in question works on this subatomic level, to cause so much supernatural mischief.

MONSIEUR MEGANIQUE

In the autumn of 1841, the north of England was afflicted with a series of dense fogs, and Liverpool was visited by the worst of them in October of that year. The Monk's Ferry railway-boat ran ashore in the deadly impenetrable mist that month, and the ferry-boats were compelled to keep their bells ringing constantly as they plied back and forth across the Mersey, to warn other vessels of their proximity.

On the Saturday evening of October 2 1841, a jade sea-fog of unusual opaqueness crept down a gas-lit Lime Street. A man in a dark green coat and a flamboyant hat sporting a jaunty feather, alighted from a carriage on that fogbound street and entered the foyer of the old Adelphi Hotel with half of his face swathed in a Persian blue silk scarf. Despite this, a few of the well-travelled guests in the Adelphi recognised the well-dressed visitor immediately; he was a supposedly genuine magician and mystic from France, known as Meganique. Some claimed he was nothing more than a charlatan, but an equal number of people swore he possessed genuine Occult powers.

A sceptical colonel who was lodging at the Adelphi is said to have challenged Meganique to give a demonstration of his 'powers' to the assembled guests and the French self-styled magician did not hesitate in accepting the challenge. Pointing to an unusual jewelled brooch on his lapel, he asked the colonel to gaze at it, which he did. The military man's five friends, who were also observing all of this, described the brooch's diamonds as flashing with a fiery rainbow light.

The colonel soon fell into a trance and Meganique concentrated on his forehead, as he read his innermost secret thoughts aloud for the benefit of the bystanders. The colonel had been having a clandestine affair with the wife of one of his friends, and that man was present in the gathering. A fight between the colonel and a fellow officer ensued and Meganique quickly made himself scarce. On the following morning, a chambermaid entered Meganique's room and caught him levitating a few feet in the air above his bed, wearing just his nightshirt. Her screams, as she dropped the bundle of clean linen she was carrying and careered off down the corridor, seemed to interfere with the magic and the occultist fell down on to the mattress in shock.

The most intriguing episode featuring the magician may interest Beatles fans. At the Royal Amphitheatre, on Great Charlotte Street (where the Royal Court now stands), there was an extravaganza being staged during the week that Meganique was in town. Well's Circus were putting on the show and two Victorian showmen about whom John Lennon would one day write a song, stunned the crowds with their acrobatic skills. Their names were William Kite and Pablo Fanque. Monsieur Fanque, the first black circus proprietor, in an age when slavery was still going strong, was also a superhuman gymnastic 'aeronaut'. He thrilled the Liverpool crowds by jumping through paper-covered hoops encircled with sharp knives, somersaulting over nine horses, and diving through flaming hogsheads, while Mr Kite somehow balanced upside down, fifty feet above the stage with a long pole pressed into the centre-part of his hair. He juggled on that pole, spun on his head, and spiralled down it as he held on to the shaft by one hand. Little did Messrs Kite and Fanque suspect that a Liverpudlian of global fame would one day pen a song about them entitled *Being for the Benefit of Mr Kite*, after coming across an old poster advertising Well's Circus in an antique shop, in 1967.

Meganique watched the show at the Amphitheatre, and being recognised by Fanque, was invited onstage. Meganique accepted and not only levitated, but apparently conjured up the shimmering green luminescent ghost that was said to haunt the theatre and very nearly caused a panic amongst the audience as a result. The phantom, which hovered centre-stage for a matter of seconds, was said to have been the ghost of a child who had drowned in the well that still exists deep beneath the clay on which the Royal Court Theatre was built.

Unlike the many stage mediums of today, who

produce no solid psychic phenomena whatsoever, and merely spout vague nonsense about 'Johns', 'Margarets' and 'Williams', Meganique delivered meaningful messages to audience members from their deceased loved ones, giving both a forename and a surname, and he even went so far as to accuse one man in the audience of being a murderer! This man bolted from the theatre, never to be seen again.

Meganique also chillingly warned Sir Philip Courtenay, MP for Bridgewater, that he would die in the Adelphi Hotel. This happened one evening as the minister challenged Meganique to give him a prediction for the New Year.

"You'll never see that year, monsieur," Meganique told Courtenay in front of several guests at a bar in the hotel. Courtenay gave a hollow laugh, but weeks later he was staying at the hotel, recuperating from a leg injury, when he accidentally overdosed on the morphine he had been prescribed to deaden the pain, and never regained consciousness.

WARNINGS FROM THE FUTURE

The following strange but true tale took place in the mid-1970s. Simon, a bright twelve-year-old who lived in Kensington, liked to build his own radio sets with electronic kits bought from Tandy's and components and bits and bobs he found on his scavenging missions to a derelict television repair shop on Tunnel Road. The boy was a wizard with transistors, capacitors, resistors — even the occasional antediluvian thermionic valve, and his 'wands' were his collection of soldering irons. Simon, whom his dull peers nicknamed 'Joe Ninety' (after the television Supermarionation puppet series), because of his closely cropped blonde hair, technical knowhow and oversized spectacles, had an uncanny knack of fixing the old radios his bin-man father brought home, having salvaged them from people's rubbish. Simon's sanctum and laboratory was the draughty attic of his

Kensington house, where a strange assortment of adapted and extended aerials and antennae protruded from the eaves. Multi-coloured spaghetti-like bunches of wires ran between old electric train transformers, salvaged gramophone loudspeakers, a discarded 1965 record player and a 1920s 'Cat's Whisker' crystal radio set that had belonged to Simon's grandfather. In that junk-filled attic of electronic contentment, Simon's happiness was derived from the sweet smell of flux vapour, as the hot solder bonded wires with its silvery alloy.

The boy was in high spirits this close July evening, after constructing an aerial booster circuit from a schematic diagram in a book he had loaned from Kensington Library. He plugged in the coaxial cable to his beloved solid state multiband VHF/AM/LW radio and inserted the other end of the thick brown wire into the socket on the circuit board of his latest project. He surveyed his handiwork one more time, to check that everything was as it should be, then took a deep breath and threw the little toggle-switch. The wire from that newly-constructed circuit board of yellow cylindrical capacitors and bead-headed transistors ran under the window and then up to the three-foot long antennae perched on the guttering of the roof.

Click! The multiband radio was switched on and Simon listened with satisfaction to the crystal-clear music and voices on his headphones. Sing Something Simple was coming through from Radio 1 loud and clear, Pete Murray's distinctive voice was on Radio 2, and as the brushed steel tuner knob was turned by careful degrees, the symphonic stringed splendour of

Mendelssohn on Radio 3, was conjured up by the forgotten magic of frequency modulation. The music was, in turn, rudely interrupted by the voice of Alastair Cooke reading yet another of his *Letters from America*, in that barely disguised Lancashire brogue that sounded as if it belonged to Oldham's Eric Sykes.

Despite his father's warnings, Simon twiddled with the tuner and the persimmon orange needle moved horizontally in fits and starts behind the square transparent frequency guide. As the needle moved to the far left of the waveband, the steady bleeps of the police transmitter could be heard. Male voices speaking in phonetic codes could also be detected. Simon knew that it was an offence to listen in to police broadcasts, because his father had told him a cautionary tale about such eavesdropping, but he was not sure if it was true, or that he had been making it up.

The story went that, a few years ago, the police allegedly put out a broadcast on their special wavebands about reports of a bag of banknotes being left under a bench in Abercromby Park. The police radio operator then told officers on the beat to visit the park, as soon as it opened in the morning. Several people who had been illegally tuning into the police had heard this broadcast, and were soon scaling the park railings. Some climbed in via the walkways around Senate House. As you probably guessed, when these eavesdroppers arrived in the park, they were all nicked for intercepting police calls. Or had this just been an urban legend, dreamt up by his dad to deter him from listening in to the police, firemen, and airline pilots? What harm could be had by just listening to the broadcasts, Simon wondered. Later that evening Simon was just about to call it a day, when he heard a very alarming message on the police waveband. "An officer has been shot!" repeated the police radio operator, several times in a row. Simon ran downstairs and dragged his father away from his armchair where he had been enjoying the highlights of that day's Wimbledon. "Sounds like you've tuned into an episode of *Kojak*, son!" he laughed, but Simon insisted the voice was English.

Simon and his father listened to the other police messages that night, but there was no further mention of any shooting. The boy felt a bit of a fool. Sometimes, in those days, VHF receivers could pick up the audio-track signal of television broadcasts, and Simon eventually started to believe that he had picked up the dialogue of some American cop show. That same night, he thought he also heard news of another shooting, again on the police frequency, this time in a jeweller's store. Simon tried to mention that to his father as well, but he ignored him and settled back down to watch the tennis.

On Wednesday, 9 July 1975, less than a week after Simon had heard the shocking police radio broadcast about an officer being shot, two policemen in Liverpool city centre approached a car that had gone through a red traffic light on Hope Street, intending to interview the driver. There were three men in the car, and they happened to be members of a highly dangerous IRA cell, who had just fled from an incident in Manchester. One of the men produced a gun and fired at one of the policemen, but missed.

The IRA members walked away from the vehicle,

but the sound of the gunshot alerted the inquiry desk sergeant at the nearby police station on Hope Street. The sergeant came out of the station to investigate the gunshot, and one of the IRA men fired another shot. The bullet struck the railing close to where the sergeant was standing and a fragment of metal, dislodged by the collision, slammed into the sergeant's chin, wounding him. The three terrorists then returned to their vehicle and drove off. The cell was later captured at a house on Oxford Road, Waterloo.

As soon as the desk sergeant was injured in the shooting, a broadcast was made on the police band to all officers. News of it was broadcast on 9 July, yet Simon had heard it days before. The other shooting the boy had heard about on his VHF signal-boosting circuit - the incident at the jeweller's - also came to pass, by a dark coincidence, on the day after the IRA incident on Hope Street. Two men carrying sawn-off shotguns in a holdall entered O'Hare's jewellery store on Breck Road, Anfield. The robbers were challenged by security guard Alfred Alcock, but one of them shot him at point-blank range, killing him instantly. The dangerous duo then fled from the murder scene in a car that was later found abandoned.

These two shootings were not connected, except in one strange way - they were both heard about days before they took place on a twelve-year-old boy's radio set in Kensington. Simon's father was so spooked by the prophetic broadcasts, he dismantled the aerial and strictly forbade his son to tune into the police frequencies, so no more signals from the future were heard in that attic.

I have investigated 'cross-time' signals before and

documented such a case in one of my books. It involved a radio operator named Billy at Merseycabs, in 1992, who heard his own voice coming over his radio one night, instructing cab drivers to pick up various fares. Every location and message Billy had heard hours before, later appeared on his computer screen, and he found himself speaking the very same sentences he had heard earlier.

One day, at the studios of Radio Merseyside, I received several telephone calls from people who had heard me talking on air about time travel and premonitions. Julie, a trainee hospital nurse, who had lodgings on Pembroke Place, told me how, in the early 1990s, she switched on her television set one evening to be confronted by a terrifying ITN newsflash: terrorists had exploded an atomic bomb in London, and stark disturbing footage of a huge mushroom cloud was shown during the report.

Having a cousin living in Bermondsey, Julie quickly rang her in a numbed state. When her cousin Anna answered, Julie told her about the newsflash, but Anna was mystified, because nothing of the kind had taken place; London was still intact. Julie told her to switch on the news and, of course, she saw no reports of any atom-bombing of London.

Imagine my surprise when a man named Neil, from Huyton, telephoned that same day and said he had been driving to his workplace in Prescot one morning, listening to BBC Radio Merseyside presenter Tony Snell on the car radio, when the programme was suddenly interrupted by a newsflash that made his stomach turn somersaults. A female presenter delivered the following grave message: "What appears to be a nuclear bomb exploded in central London ten minutes ago. Reports of widespread devastation are coming in as I speak. The Houses of Parliament, and possibly Buckingham Palace, are reported to have been destroyed."

Someone, possibly Tony Snell, gasped, and said, "No," and then the programme reverted to normal. Neil was so shaken by the shocking broadcast, he pulled over, and almost vomited. He drove to a car park and listened to the news on the car radio, but there was no mention of any nuclear explosion in the capital. When he finally reached his workplace, thirty minutes late, he told his boss what he had heard, but his explanations just seemed like a weak excuse for his lateness. Nevertheless, to humour him, since he did look a bit green, he suggested that perhaps some radio play on another frequency had drifted on to the same frequency as the Tony Snell Show, but Neil was not to be fobbed off, he knows what he heard and, to this day, he prays that his 'premonition' will not come true.

SNAKES ALIVE

The night this strange and frightening incident happened to Rita Boxwood was easy to recall: Halloween - 31 October 1958 - which fell on a Friday that year. Twenty-two-year-old Rita, from Toxteth, left her home on Grove Street at around 6.30pm and went to pay a visit to her friend Nancy Flannegan on Cardwell Street, Edge Hill. Once there, Rita played traditional Halloween Night games with Nancy and her two teenaged sisters for almost an hour and a half. A row of scrumptious-looking apples had been hung from a doorframe by tying string to their stalks, and Rita, Nancy and her sisters had fun trying to bite into them with their teeth and without using their hands. Another game followed, which also involved trying to bite apples, only this time they were bobbing about in a tin washtub full of water, and they had their hands behind their backs, as they attempted to snatch them with their mouths.

Chestnuts were roasted in the oven that night, some of which exploded, creating a mess in the oven, because Nancy had forgotten to prick their skins with a fork. Being Halloween, Nancy told a few silly ghost stories, but by around 7.30pm, Rita sat down with the Flannegan family in their living-room and everyone turned their attention to the modern storyteller - the television. The new seventeen-inch black and white Murphy television warmed up and everyone sat back to enjoy the then popular hospital drama, *Emergency Ward 10*. After that programme had ended, Rita left the Flannegan's house, even though Nancy had asked her to stay by telling her that the equally popular game show, *Take Your Pick* was just about to start.

Rita left anyway and decided to call on her cousin Joan, who lived on Hall Lane, Kensington. She walked up Queensland Street, crossed sloping Grinfield Street (then known, for some reason, as 'The Broo' - a Scots word meaning the brow of a hill), and then Rita hurried down Mason Street, which, in the 1950s, was rather poorly lit for much of its length. As she passed Shimmin Street, she noticed two mongrel dogs barking furiously as they peered down a grid. A small child stood about five feet away from the noisy canines holding a stick, and he too was staring at the grid. By his feet rested the metal grille that had covered the hole in the gutter. Rita guessed that they were looking at a rat, but then something happened which was to give her nightmares for many years to come.

A massive snake's head emerged from the hole in one terrifyingly rapid motion. The head was the size of a large pear, and the section of its curved body which was visible formed an arch, as the creature darted forward twice in rapid succession, attempting to bite the mongrels with its impossibly wide mouth and two dangerous-looking fangs. One of the dogs emitted a high-pitched yelp then slunk off down the gloomy street. The young boy did not like the look of the snake at close quarters either. He screamed and fled round the corner into Shimmin Street, crying for his mother.

The fur on the back of the braver mongrel stood on end, and it snarled threateningly as it snapped its little mouth at the formidable snake. A second or two later it must have thought better of tackling such a fearsome adversary and suddenly bolted towards Rita, whose legs had already turned to jelly; she had a long-standing phobia of snakes. The dog sped off past her, as the rest of the snake's body slithered out of the grid. It came crawling towards her at a remarkable speed.

Rita tried to scream, but was so mesmerised by the snake, all she could muster was a faint strangled cry. She felt as if she was moving in slow motion, as she tried to get away from the thing, and fully expected the snake's venom-filled fangs to sink into her ankles at any moment. Now that its whole length was visible, she realised that it was far bigger than it had originally looked. About six feet in length and immensely powerful, it was rapidly closing in on her.

A car suddenly swung into Mason Street from Irvine Street, and its headlamps momentarily dazzled Rita. She dashed out into the road with tears of terror streaming from her eyes, and the driver of the oncoming car sounded his horn continuously and screeched to a halt a foot away from what would have been a fatal impact. Rita scrambled on to the vehicle's bonnet and the infuriated driver got out of the car, ready to give her a piece of his mind, but then he saw the snake - and what a snake!

The scaly body of the huge out-of-place reptile suddenly contracted and came to a halt. Its cold yellow-green eyes studied them both, in a moment of indecision, then it turned and slithered away from then along the gutter. The driver, Billy Marsten, helped Rita into his car and drove her home. One the way, he stopped and called over to a policeman on Oxford Street and told him about the snake, but he showed little interest.

Over the years since that eventful Halloween night, there have been several rumours about snakes being at large in the sewers under Mason Street and parts of Crown Street. If the scare stories are to be believed, it raises the question of how the snakes got there in the first place. Well, a little research on my part has uncovered the following snippet of intriguing information.

In February 1870, William Cross, a colourful, if rather eccentric, naturalist, ordered a consignment of serpents to be brought over from the West Indies to Liverpool.

Amongst the specimens was a fully grown female python, and during the sea passage to the port, this snake gave birth to no less than thirty-five miniature pythons. Mr Cross somehow managed to transport all of these snakes to his home on Mason Street without a customs official noticing the dangerous imports. Cross kept the snakes in his back yard, which adjoined the stables of John Henderson, a ship-store dealer, and the adult python was housed in a strong specially-constructed cage. Nevertheless, in the early hours of Wednesday, 9 February 1870, the large serpent somehow managed to burrow its way through the base board of its enclosure and wriggle through an aperture in the fence, thus gaining access to Mr Henderson's stable-yard.

At 7am that morning, a carter entered the yard and came upon an horrific, almost surreal sight. The python was tightly coiled right around the belly of Mr Henderson's horse, which was kicking its legs against the wooden sides of its stall and shrieking wildly in an attempt to shake off the gigantic reptile. During the life-and-death struggle, this unnatural fight was surprisingly won by the horse, which eventually managed to bite the python's head off. The headless body writhed about on the stone floor of the stable as the hysterical steed's hooves stamped upon it again and again, sending its bloody innards spraying out across the cobbled yard.

The plucky horse survived the attack, even though it had sustained a very nasty-looking snake bite on its back. Mr Henderson was livid, and warned Cross that he would take legal action unless he kept his "accursed menagerie" under better control in the future.

However, not long afterwards, more snakes escaped from Cross's yard, and some seem to have made a beeline for the sewers, where there lived a plentiful supply of fat succulent sewer rats, just waiting to be eaten.

Is it possible that the descendants of careless Mr Cross's escaped snakes could be responsible for the reports of the serpents in Mason Street and Crown Street over the years? The last report of a snake under

Mason Street was made in the 1960s, when two tramps found access to a tunnel which led to the cellar of a local pub and a lemonade bottling works in Edge Hill. This tunnel was, without a doubt, part of the subterranean labyrinth created by the 'Edge Hill Mole' Joseph Williamson (1769-1840), the compulsive tunneller of that district. The tramps routinely used the tunnel to steal crates of beer and lemonade, but one afternoon they were allegedly chased by a huge snake during one of their underground pilfering expeditions. A policeman apprehended one of the vagrants and dismissed his tale about a giant snake as a typical figment of a brain pickled in alcohol!

Some people believe that Williamson's tunnels were used for smuggling after his demise. James Stonehouse, nineteenth century historian and author, states in his book, *The Streets of Liverpool* (1869), that the vaults and passageways left neglected after the death of the Mole of Edge Hill, were quite possibly used for various unlawful purposes. Stonehouse also relates how a friend living on Mason Street once told him that he and his family had been startled to hear the most awful screams and yells underneath their home, where the vaults are located. There was an investigation of the vaults on the following day but nothing amiss was found in the Stygian gloom. Were the screams of a supernatural origin, or just the high-spirited shrieks of a bunch of subterranean smugglers? We will probably never know.

VOICES ACROSS THE MERSEY

The belief that the full moon holds some sort of influence over us is a very ancient one, and over the years, research has been carried out to see if there is any truth in this hoary old notion. The fact that the human body is made up of seventy per cent water, means that the gravitational field of the moon - which is powerful enough to influence the tides of the world - must also affect the fluids of the body, on a microscopic scale.

Then, of course, there are the numerous studies which seem to confirm that crank telephone calls and domestic arguments peak at the time of the full moon. A recent study at Leeds University found that GPs in the UK are likely to see thirty thousand more patients on the day after a full moon, thought to be because of some unexplained effect the moon has on hypochondriacs. Casualty unit admissions at hospitals also seem to increase at full lunation.

In the world of the paranormal, the moon, particularly when it is full, has always been associated with witchcraft and sorcery and for centuries it has traditionally been cited as the source of witches' power. The moon's phases also determine the esbats and circles of the witch.

In 1965, the late neurologist and inventor Andrija Puharich carried out an experiment regarding the phases and position of the moon and incidences of telepathy. Puharich discovered that telepathic contact between individuals seemed to be strongest at the time of the full moon. Other studies into the same phenomenon seemed to indicate that our natural satellite's gravitational forces, coupled with its luminance at full moon, are somehow conducive to telepathy.

I can recall a case that was reported to me many years ago, which seems to back up Puharich's findings. At precisely 4.10am, on 15 February 1995, a full moon hung over Cheshire. At Great Sutton, a woman named Sheila heard her daughter Cathy shouting to her. She went to the window but could see no one in the street below. Yet she was so sure she had heard Cathy's voice that she went downstairs in her nightgown, convinced that she must be around somewhere outside. Her husband also got up, curious as to what she was up to. Sheila opened the front door and looked out into the wintry street. Not a soul was about. "I'm sure I heard our Cathy just now," she told her husband Geoff.

"She's in Liverpool with him. You know that," said Geoff, struggling to keep his tired bloodshot eyes open. 'Him' was Cathy's boyfriend, a young layabout who was always cadging money off Geoff. He went back upstairs, and as he got halfway up, Sheila called out, "There! Listen!"

Geoff stopped and listened. He could hear nothing, but he came back downstairs when he saw his wife open the front door and set off down the short garden path to go in search of her daughter. She had definitely heard Cathy shout "Mum!" and had then heard her sobbing. All her maternal instincts screamed out to her that something was wrong. Her daughter needed her, but where was she? Why couldn't she see her? "Cathy!" she cried, every nerve in her body straining with anxiety. When Sheila had walked down the street and back looking in every garden and behind every hedge, she had to accept that Cathy was not anywhere near the house. She was very reluctant to give up the search, but what could she do? She could no longer hear Cathy's voice and she was getting more and more chilled in the wintry street. Geoff kept on calling for Sheila to come back inside, out of the cold, and she eventually did so, albeit reluctantly. Rationally, she was satisfied that Cathy was not anywhere near the house, although something inside her would not allow her to believe this, much as she wanted to. With the memory of Cathy's voice still replaying inside her head, she finally gave up and went back to bed.

At 9am, Cathy turned up at the house with a heavily bandaged head. Geoff and Sheila guessed immediately who was responsible for her injury; they had been half-expecting just such an outcome, ever since she had started going out with her violent boyfriend. It had been pure agony for them watching her fall for the wrong type of man, but they had been powerless to stop it. Now their worst nightmare had come to pass.

They soon learned the whole sorry tale. Cathy and her boyfriend had gone to a Valentine's Day house-party. They had been enjoying themselves until a man started dancing with Cathy, then things turned nasty. Her boyfriend had attacked the man in a fit of jealousy and had been thrown out of the house - along with Cathy. On their way home, at four o'clock in the morning, he had accused her of being unfaithful, and had punched her and then pushed her over. Cathy gashed her head on a street bollard, after which her boyfriend had stormed off. She had walked the streets of Everton on her own, in a daze, with blood pouring down her face, crying out for her mum, just as Sheila had heard. Even stranger, Cathy had heard her mother shout her name in reply, and for a time had been convinced that she had come over to help her from Great Sutton, but she was unable to find her. Not long afterwards a passer-by had found her and telephoned for an ambulance. The gash on her head needed five stitches.

When mother and daughter compared notes about the events of that night, Geoff wanted to put it all down to coincidence, but Sheila knew better. She had inherited her gift from her grandmother, who was very telepathic. Even more telling, was the fact that her grandmother had told her that the powers of the mind increased at full moon - and there had been one that morning.

LUNAR TELEPATHY

Going back over more than a century, to 1884, we come to another case of so-called 'Lunar Telepathy'. On Monday, 17 December 1883, John Fitz, a groom of St-Martin-in-the-Fields, Chester, married a beautiful, young and respectable woman named Elizabeth, after only nine months of a whirlwind courtship. John had seemed such a kind, loving, gentle man, at first, but after the honeymoon in Wales, he underwent a drastic change in his personality. He became very possessive towards Elizabeth, and when she happened to mention a very good friend of hers named Charles, whom she had known platonically in Liverpool two years ago, John Fitz instantly flew into a frightening rage, and forbade any mention of his name in his presence again.

At 10.30pm, on the Sunday night of 24 February 1884, as Elizabeth was preparing for bed, her husband suddenly produced a cut-throat razor and calmly asked her if she was ready to die. The young woman recoiled in shock, and gasped, "No, no I am not." Her deranged husband had once again been imagining that his wife did not care for him, and was consumed with jealousy. Nevertheless, he somehow managed to regain control of his emotions and put the razor away in a box. Elizabeth lay awake all that night, and planned to make a dash from the house at the earliest opportunity. On the following morning, she hid the box containing the razor, intending to seize the first chance to escape. However, her husband's mood had softened somewhat during the night, and over breakfast she saw flashes of the old John Fitz. She tried to convince herself that his behaviour on the previous night had been an aberration and she decided to stay put in the house, out of sympathy for him.

However, she soon regretted her decision, because his jealousy soon reared its ugly head again and he angrily demanded to know where the razor was. When she admitted that it was hidden downstairs, John told her through gritted teeth, "I am going to cut your throat and my own too, and I will explain in writing exactly what I have done it for."

As soon as his back was turned, Elizabeth grabbed an Ulster coat and rushed out of the house via the back door. She scaled a ten-foot wall, topped with shards of broken glass, and only managed to get over it by putting the folded Ulster underneath her. She then hid in an outhouse next door, where she was later discovered by a neighbour, cringing in terror in a corner.

From there, Elizabeth made her way to her brother's house, and he, in turn, summoned the police. When questioned, John Fitz told detectives he had only been joking and "wouldn't harm a hair on dear Elizabeth's head". He begged for his wife to come back home with him, but that was out of the question, and she stayed at her brother's. Believe it or not, John Fitz was only charged twelve pounds to keep the peace for three months!

At midnight, on 10 April that year - the night of the full moon - Elizabeth Fitz was in bed at her brother's house, with tears stinging her eyes. Her young life was now blighted, and she could scarcely remember the young carefree girl she had been just weeks before. She gazed sorrowfully at the full moon, whose brilliant silvery light was flooding in though the window, when all of a sudden, she thought of Charles Llewellyn, the Liverpool man she had been fond of two years ago. The image of Charles's gentle face suddenly appeared on the disc of the full moon. Elizabeth got up from the bed, fascinated by the strange spectacle, and walked to the window with a quizzical smile.

At that precise moment, miles away across the Mersey, Charles Llewellyn was also having difficulty sleeping. The bachelor had many business problems on his mind, which were keeping him awake. He sat up in bed and chanced to look up at the lunar orb, which had never looked more beautiful. The eerie female features on the moon's surface made him do a double take. Surely it could not be ... but yes ... it was the face of Elizabeth, the woman he had hoped to marry, a couple of years ago. Rather than read any romantic significance into the vision, he simply took it as proof of his weary, overtaxed mind craving sleep and he sighed deeply; how different his troubles would seem with Elizabeth by his side.

Elizabeth made a note of the lunar mystery in her diary, and Charles also did the same in his, but neither attached too much significance to what they had seen; they both merely put it down to their unhappy state of mind. Then, a few months later, fate suddenly threw the couple together again. They met in a street in Chester, seemingly by chance, and this time, Charles was determined not to let Elizabeth slip away from his grasp. Elizabeth sought a divorce from her husband and Charles married her later that year. During their courtship they discovered that each had seen the other's face on the moon that April night, and that inexplicable incident only served to reinforce their love.

LONELY HEARTS

In April 1897, the following message appeared in the personal column of a Liverpool newspaper:

Lady, 32, well-educated, wishes to make the acquaintance of a gentleman requiring a home-loving companion. Genuine.

Philip Brown, a fifty-five-year-old bachelor, read the notice, and quickly sent off a reply. The 'lady' replied in the newspaper column to 'Philip':

Dear Friend,

I was so pleased to read your letter, as I have not yet had the happiness to meet the man I could love. I am very fond of music, and am told I play the piano and harp exceedingly well. My hair is dark and I am 33 years of age next August. I will tell you about my father and mother when I see you. I have a little money in the bank, and a number of shares in some collieries, which give me good income. Please meet me outside the Town Hall on

Castle Street tomorrow (Tuesday) at eleven; wear lilies of the valley in your coat, as I love those flowers, and carry a handkerchief in your hand. Keep wiping your hat with it, so I may know you are waiting for me. I will wear a blue dress.

Yours very sincerely, Kathleen Eastwood

Philip duly turned up at the Town Hall at 11 o'clock that Tuesday morning, with a spray of lily of the valley pinned to his lapel and a handkerchief in his hand. About one hundred and fifty young fellows from the Cotton Exchange congregated at the corner of Dale Street and Castle Street, with the object of watching developments.

The man in search of a wife and soulmate walked up and down in front of the Town Hall, wiping his hat now and then, and smiling at any woman passing who happened to be wearing a blue dress. For half an hour this went on, providing great amusement for the growing crowd on the other side of Dale Street. More and more passers-by who had had the hoax explained to them joined the multitude, and even a policeman who had come to disperse the crowd, upon hearing the reasons behind the stifled laughter, joined in their cruel game.

At last, a kindly old man was told of what was going on and he crossed the road and pulled at Philip's arm, urging him to move on. He then had a quiet word with him and told him that the letter in the newspaper had been written by a hoaxer.

"I'm afraid you're being made fun of," said the tearful old man, a widower who knew what it meant to live without love. Philip could barely take it in, then he noticed the sea of jeering faces across the road.

"Have you seen your girl yet, old chappie?" shouted one of the crowd.

"Go now," advised the old man.

The lily of the valley fell from Philip's lapel, and was trampled underfoot by the jackals and hyenas who followed him up Castle Street, hurling cruel quips: "Have you given up on her?" one shouted; "Have you found your wife, old man?" bellowed another.

The crowd pursued Philip as far as Bold Street, where, thankfully, a hansom cab stopped and whisked him away from their taunts to his large empty home on Huskisson Street. He had never felt lonelier in his life as he stood in the cold hallway. What a fool he had been to think that he might find love with a woman almost half his age. He deserved to be ridiculed. These, and a multitude of other negative thoughts began to crowd his mind until he could stand it no longer. There was no joy in his life and he had nothing left to live for, he might as well put himself out of his misery and end it all.

A bone-weary numbness enveloped Philip as he walked like a zombie into the drawing room, where he took an eight-ounce bottle of chloroform from a drawer in his bureau, and got ready to pour the contents into a sofa-cushion. It would just be like going to sleep, he reasoned, and the idea felt very comforting. He sat himself down in his favourite armchair and uncorked the bottle, but his cat, Simon, jumped on his knee and began purring softly. His little feline friend seemed so pleased to see him, and kept on rubbing its face against his chin.

The sensation of touching another living being is a very powerful force and it broke through the cloak of melancholy which had brought Philip to the point of suicide. He looked down at the trusting face of his beloved pet, and stepped back from the brink. He just could not bring himself to abandon the poor animal. He pushed the cork back into the bottle and put it back in the drawer. The little cat seemed to sense that his master was in dire need of affection and nestled down in the crook of his folded arms.

Philip sat for a long time like this in his fireside armchair dwelling on those pitiless jeering faces on Dale Street. What a fool he had been. Would he ever find someone to share his life with? He had tried so many times over the years, but Cupid had never helped him one iota.

Simon presently jumped out of his arms and curled up by his feet on the hearthrug. Philip dozed off and soon found himself in the midst of a bizarre dream. Clouds of soot were erupting from the fireplace, and a strange screeching sound was coming down the chimney. Everything in the room was blackened with soot, pierced by a few narrow shafts of sunlight shining through the carboniferous chaos.

What happened next was the typical stuff of dreams: a goose flew out of the unlit fireplace and was just visible as a pale ghostly bird flapping its wings frantically as it circled the room. The surreal scene included the outline of a woman sitting in the armchair opposite. She was crying out in alarm at the sudden arrival of the sooty goose and the ruination of all the soft furnishings.

As the clouds of black powder and grey ash started

to thin, Philip could see that the woman was beautiful. Despite the soot on her face, she was a fine-looking woman with large attractive eyes. She looked strangely familiar, but the mask of soot made it difficult to determine exactly who she was.

Philip woke up and looked straight at the fireplace, half expecting to see the sooty goose, but the parlour was as neat and tidy as ever, with nothing amiss. Philip wondered what the significance of the dream could be, if indeed it had any, for this was in the age before Freud and dream analysis, when dreams were often interpreted supernaturally. The dream provided a fitting end to a horrible day he would rather forget, and he soon put it to the back of his mind.

Something very odd happened a few days later. Philip Brown's cousin Ralph sent him an invitation to a civic ball, which was to be held at St George's Hall in a week's time. The invitation was for Philip and a friend. Philip flung the invitation on the fire, as it only served to underline the fact that he had no lady friend, but before the coals could consume it, he suddenly grabbed the brass coal tongues and retrieved it. He pictured the laughing faces in Dale Street in his mind's eye and clenched his jaw. He would show them!

The grey-haired bachelor went over to his writing desk and began to formulate a plan to find a suitable specimen of the fairer sex to take to the ball. He wrote the heading, 'places to meet females' and beneath it scribbled the words, 'libraries, shops, parks'. But the ball was in a week's time, so how on earth could was he going to meet a lady and then ask her to the ball? It was beyond the bounds of Victorian decency to become so familiar in so short a time.

Wait a moment! From the depths of Philip's fevered mind, a woman's face suddenly materialised - Elizabeth Barratt, who worked behind the china counter in Bunney's. Philip had spent a lot of time in the Bunney's store over the past year, buying all sorts of birthday and Christmas gifts for his five aunts. He had soon noticed the lovely Miss Barratt, and learned of her name from his friend Alfred, who had once courted her cousin. Philip lost no time in visiting the Church Street store. On the first day, Elizabeth was nowhere to be seen, but on the following day she was back at her usual counter in the china goods section, looking as beautiful and radiant as ever.

Every time Philip's courage failed him and he started to hesitate, he would conjure up the mocking faces of the mob on Dale Street. He braced himself; a sharp intake of breath, and suddenly, unbelievably, he was walking towards Miss Barratt. He fidgeted with his gloves, made small talk, his words coming out all muddled, but he knew by the blush on her cheeks and the way she looked at him with her eyes that he was in with a chance. He told her about the civic ball at St George's Hall, and eventually plucked up the courage to ask her if she would do him the great honour of accompanying him to the event. There! it was out, he had actually managed it!

To his amazement, the delightful creature nodded shyly, and seemed to lose her voice for a moment before she recovered it with a gentle cough. Philip almost skipped back to Huskisson Street that day and could barely contain himself waiting for the big day to arrive. But would she actually come? and if she did, would they enjoy each other's company? He need not have worried. The evening of the ball was a dream, and by December, Elizabeth and Philip were engaged to be married. One of the first things Elizabeth noticed when visiting Philip's residence, was that the chimney to his parlour fireplace desperately needed cleaning, because every time there was a strong wind, flecks of soot would come down the chimney. Mr Grant, his usual sweep, was not available due to illness, so Elizabeth suggested her cousin, Rory Kinnear, who was a bit of a jack of all trades and a self-taught expert on the cleaning of chimneys. He would only charge six shillings, instead of the usual ten that most sweeps charged.

It was arranged that Rory would sweep the chimney on the following Saturday morning, whilst Philip and Elizabeth were out shopping. However, the couple returned home at noon, expecting to find the work complete, only to find Rory up on the roof, clinging to the chimney stack for dear life, as clouds of soot were issuing from the chimney pot. Elizabeth was about to wave to her cousin, but Philip warned that such a distraction could prove fatal, so the couple entered the house as unobtrusively as possible.

Philip's maid of all work, Mrs O'Brien met them by the front door, where she had been waiting anxiously for them to return. She was in a bit of a flap, because there were strange noises conning from the fireplace in the parlour. Philip and Elizabeth rushed to investigate and found a tarpaulin laid out on the hearthrug. Simon the cat was keeping well out of harm's way in the doorway, his ears twitching at the unearthly racket.

Strange shrieks came down the chimney, followed by a massive cloud of soot which took the couple by complete surprise. As Simon fled upstairs, Elizabeth fell back into an armchair and vanished with the rest of the parlour into the filthy black cloud. Philip suddenly realised, with a sense of deja vu, that he had witnessed this very scene months before, in April, when he had had that peculiar dream, and so he knew exactly what to expect next. Sure enough, a loud noise from the chimney heralded the arrival of the goose, which flapped its way out of the fireplace in yet another billowing cloud of foul-tasting dust.

It soon became apparent that Rory Kinnear did not have the first clue about cleaning chimneys, in fact, he did not even possess a sweep's brush. Instead, he had decided to resort to an old chimney-cleaning trick that was common in the country, in which a goose was simply dropped down the chimney. The frenzied beating of unwitting bird's wings as it descended, were a surprisingly efficient, if cruel, way to clean out the layers of soot. Animal rights were plainly not an issue in those days! Philip was not at all angry at Rory Kinnear's incompetence, because he was more intrigued by his strange dream coming true than the mess in his parlour, and at least the chimney must now be well swept! He smiled as he looked at Elizabeth's comical blackened face. Yes, it had been her face he had seen in that dream back in April and how his life had improved since then! A bit of soot was nothing to a man who had found such unexpected happiness so late in life.

In the following year, Philip married Elizabeth and the couple then moved to Yorkshire and eventually became the parents of six children.

A WEST DERBY HAUNTING

Ghosts that cause harm are thankfully very rare, but I remember one case, a few years ago, in which a man died from a heart attack after being chased through his Anfield home by the ghost of a girl. I have myself been harmed by a poltergeist (a nail was driven through my left hand) and then there was the case, many years ago, in which a poltergeist left a priest needing eight stitches to his head, when a large television set was thrown at him. The following story is about another of these violent manifestations.

In March 2008, Greg, a twenty-eight-year-old security guard, moved to a flat in West Derby, close to Mab Lane. Greg was originally from Bootle, but had moved after separating from his partner, Ashley. As a result of the traumatic time he had gone through with Ashley, he vowed never to live with anyone again for the foreseeable future.

Nevertheless, by the middle of March, with the promise of Spring in the air, the security guard could not help noticing a beautiful girl who worked in a certain shop on Church Street, in the city centre. He plucked up the courage to ask her out for a drink, and to his surprise, she accepted at once. The girl's name was Emma. By April, twenty-six-year-old Emma was already talking about settling down with someone, and this made Greg a little wary of how seriously he was getting involved with her, so soon after his split with Ashley. One half of his mind was saying, "Come on, Greg, you're approaching thirty, and she's the one," whilst the other half was warning him to keep Emma at arm's length, at least for now. After all, had Ashley not seemed equally wonderful at the beginning of their relationship?

Early one evening, in his new West Derby flat, Greg fell asleep on the sofa; he often enjoyed a nap before starting his night shift. He dreamed that Ashley was kissing his face and stroking his shoulder, but when he woke up, at around 10pm, the lounge was in darkness - and he could still feel someone's lips pressing on his mouth. A moment later, the kissing sensation suddenly went away. Greg groped for the lamp and switched it on and swore when he saw the time. Why hadn't the alarm clock gone off? He had set it for 8.30pm, as he had to be in work for 10pm sharp. He saw that the button had been pressed down to cancel the alarm, but he knew that he hadn't done it. He had definitely set it before his nap and he had not touched it since.

He drove like a madman to his workplace in the city centre, and only at 1.30am, during a break in his rounds, did he have time to dwell on that strange kiss he had felt after waking from the dream of Ashley. He asked his workmate, an older man named Clark, if he had ever had sensations from a dream which overlapped into his waking life. Clark grinned and said, "Oh, yeah! I've dreamt I was making love to a woman and woken to find myself kissing the pillow. Woke up drooling another time, after I bit my tongue. I'd been dreaming I was eating a Meatball Marinana sandwich in Subway."

"No, listen, this really was happening to me ... I was still being kissed after I'd woken up."

"What're you complaining about, mate? That's not so bad is it?" laughed Clark, and then turned his attention back to the CCTV monitor, as he drank from a can of Red Bull.

The next day, at 4pm, Greg was in the shower, when he thought he heard his landline telephone ringing in the lounge. He slipped out of the shower, and poked his head out of the bathroom doorway, listening. "Must be next door's phone," he said to himself, as he could no longer hear the telephone ringing. Suddenly feeling chilled, he hurried back into the shower and started singing under the hot invigorating jet of water.

Emma, meanwhile, was at her home on Queen's Drive, Walton, feeling a little shocked. With her mobile phone pressed to her ear, she listened to an unknown female voice who had answered Greg's phone. "He's in the shower," was all this woman had to say.

"Oh ... right ... erm ... could you tell him Emma called then?" she said, feeling a cold lump of foreboding swelling in her throat.

The woman hung up without a word of reply.

When Emma told her mother what had just happened, she told her not to jump to conclusions; there was probably a perfectly innocent explanation for what had happened. "Has he got a sister, for example?" she asked.

Emma shook her head, too choked up to say a word, because Greg had told her he was an only child.

"Are you sure you dialled the right number?" Emma's mum asked. "It's easily done to get just one digit wrong ... I've done it myself many a time."

"Look, Mum, it was definitely the right number."

"Oh Emma, love. You're probably worrying yourself over nothing. He's not the two-timing type. I can spot those types a mile off. I know I've only met him once, but he seemed really genuine to me."

Emma's mother put the kettle on and smiled reassuringly at her daughter, but Emma could see it was forced. It was obvious that she now had doubts about Greg as well.

Emma decided not to try phoning him again, scared that it might confirm her worst fears. So she waited until he called her at 6.30pm, and she was very cool towards him -something he picked up on immediately, from the flat tone of her voice. "What's wrong?" he asked.

Emma decided to confront him head on. "Who was that woman who answered the phone when I rang this afternoon?" There! It was out. She had really fallen for Greg and was not at all sure she really wanted to know the answer to her question.

"Eh? What are you talking about?" said Greg, taken aback.

He's obviously a good liar, thought Emma to herself.

"I phoned you this afternoon and a woman answered and said you were in the shower." Emma's voice was now full of derision, certain that he had been two-timing her.

"Emma, there's no woman here. You must've called the wrong number, babe."

"Don't 'babe' me ... I hate that word ... goodbye." With that she hung up.

Greg called back immediately. "Emma, I swear on my father's grave, no woman was here today."

That made Emma stop and think; in the short time she had known Greg, she had gathered that he had worshipped his late father; he was always talking about him and celebrating all the things he had done in his life. And yet, she knew she had not dialled the wrong number, as she had Greg's phone number stored in her mobile, and she was sure she had not pressed some other stored number - or had she?

She was now beginning to doubt herself. She suddenly found herself saying, "Okay, I'm sorry for doubting you," and she then timidly whispered that she loved him.

He did not reciprocate by saying that he loved her too - he avoided saying things like that nowadays - but she could tell he was very upset, because she had half-accused him of being unfaithful.

On the following day, Greg took Emma to an out of town shopping centre, and as they made their way back to his flat in a taxi, Emma suggested they should stop off at a pub and have a relaxing drink. Greg agreed it was a great idea, and asked the cab driver if he could take them to the nearest pub and he soon pulled up outside the Bulldog, on Leyfield Road. In a corner of this pub, Greg poured out his heart, and explained why he had never told Emma that he loved her, even though he truly did, and that he was scared to jump in at the deep end, after the big break-up with 'her' - meaning Ashley. "But I tell you what, Emma; I wish I'd met you instead of her all those years back. We'd probably have a few kids and a semi in Knotty Ash by now," Greg told her, looking down at the rising slow-motion bubbles in his pint of lager.

Emma hugged him and had to struggle to hold back the tears. Then she beamed a beautiful smile. "Why Knotty Ash?" she laughed. "What's so special about it?"

"I don't know, I just always thought it would be great to have an address with Knotty Ash in it. It sounds so funny."

An hour later they were making love in Greg's bed, which was where something very worrying took place. The bed started shaking, and no, it was not the two lovers that were causing the effect!

"Greg! What's happening?" shrieked Emma, clinging to him as the bed turned clockwise by about forty degrees, then juddered to a halt.

Greg swore and he and Emma sat up, looking at the bed and then at one another with shocked expressions. He made a feeble joke about feeling the earth move, but Emma was not amused. She had found the whole thing deeply disturbing and she leapt out of bed and started to dress.

"What're you doing, Em? You're not going, are you?"

"Yes, I'm going home," Emma told him, then jumped to one side. "Ouch!" she cried. "Something's just pinched my leg. Look at it!"

Greg could see the red mark just above her knee. "Well, I didn't do it, if that's what you're thinking," he said.

"I know you didn't... there's a ghost in here," said Emma buttoning up her blouse up wrongly in her rush to get her clothes on.

Greg repositioned the bed and then got dressed himself. He pulled on a pair of jeans, a tee shirt and his moccasin slippers, and as he hunted for his car keys, he felt cold fingers stroke his face. By then, Emma was already in the hallway. She had turned very pale and even though her fingers were feeling her left earlobe for a lost earring, she did not stop to look for it because the ghost had really freaked her out.

"Hang on a minute, I don't know where my car keys are," said Greg, looking down the side and back of his bedside cabinet where he had left them.

"I'll be outside!" said Emma and left the hallway without waiting for a reply.

After several minutes' of frantic searching, Greg finally located his keys - they were in his kitchen cupboard for some bizarre reason, even though he knew for a fact that he had not put them there. He tried to open the front door, but it seemed to be stuck and would not budge. He twisted the handle this way and that but the door felt as if it were locked. He lifted the flap of the letterbox and could see Emma standing in a blustery wind next to his car.

"I can't open the door!" he shouted to her. She came over and stooped down so that her eyes met his through the letterbox.

"You're kidding," she said, straightening up. She

could see Greg through the frosted glass of the front door - and she could also see the fuzzy outline of someone approaching behind him from the end of the hallway. "Who's the heck's that?" she shouted through the letterbox.

"Who's what? What are you talking about, Emma?" Greg shouted back, his voice muffled somewhat as the flap of the letterbox dropped down.

The handle of the front door twisted violently of its own accord and the door shook as Greg shouted Emma's name. To Emma's horror, she could see a woman grappling with him through the frosted glass; a woman with a livid snow-white face, contrasting sharply with her mop of curly red hair. Emma grabbed hold of the door handle and screamed out at the top of her voice. She rammed the door with every ounce of her strength, and it eventually shot open to reveal Greg standing a few feet down the hall, with his arms outstretched, as if he were fighting off someone - or something.

"Get off! Get off!" he screamed. "Emma, help me ... do something ... please."

Emma grabbed hold of him, and pulled him towards the front door. Just as they were crossing the threshold, something snatched at a lock of her long hair and tugged it with such force, that her scalp felt as if it were being torn. Emma let out a string of expletives and lashed out at whatever was behind her with her left fist, whilst still clinging on to Greg with her other hand. Her valiant efforts paid off when the thing finally released her hair.

Without a backward glance, the couple fled from the house, jumped into the car, and tore off down the road, knowing they had left the front door wide open. At the end of the road, Greg suddenly regained a modicum of courage and decided to reverse the vehicle, so that he could go and lock up, despite Emma pleading with him to take her home and not go back.

Greg argued that he could not just leave the door unlocked; he might have all his stuff stolen and he was not prepared to take the risk. He got out of the car and cautiously approached the entrance to the flat, then took a deep breath before attempting to close the door. As he put his hand on the doorknocker, something invisible was heard to run down the hallway, screeching with laughter as it flew towards him. It wrapped itself around him and held him in a vice-like embrace, even though he staggered backwards into the street. He pounded his own chest as he tried to beat it off, but it would not free him from its clutches. Then he felt those icy lips on his face again; those same lips he had felt that night when he had awakened in the darkness. The lips traced the contours of his face and slid over to his ear. "I'm buried in Yewtree," giggled the entity's voice. "Does that put you off, love?"

"Greg, what's wrong?" Emma shouted over to him as she left the car. She could see him standing on the path with a look of petrified horror on his face.

"In the name of the Father, and of the Son ..." Greg recited, as he made the sign of the cross, "... and of the Holy Ghost, Amen!"

At these words, the entity's inhuman strength seemed to evaporate and it slithered to the ground. A heartbeat later, the front door slammed shut, all by itself. Emma took hold of Greg's hand and guided him gently back to the car, and as she did so, she noticed the net curtains of the lounge window twitch slightly, as if someone was watching them, even though she knew that the lounge was empty. She even thought she saw a pallid face come into view behind those curtains. She shuddered, relieved to be out of the haunted flat.

The couple drove off at speed, and not until they had put several miles between themselves and Greg's flat, were they able to breathe more easily. Nothing would have persuaded Greg to return to that flat in West Derby, even to collect his things. His friend Clark and another man kindly offered to go and collect them for him, and both said that something had spat at them as they walked down the hallway carrying his television set to their van. Clark also noted that his radio had been smashed to bits and a number of plates had been shattered on the kitchen floor.

Greg was so badly shaken up by his ordeal that he had to stay off work for a month and suffered terrible nightmares about the ghost. He also had an asthma attack one night, after waking up from one particularly bad dream.

A neighbour of the haunted flat says the ghost is that of a middle-aged woman who died after a long and painful illness in the 1980s. She was buried at Yewtree Cemetery, which is not too far from the haunted residence. This neighbour told me how, one night, when he was reading the Echo in his living-room, he suddenly became aware of a faint noise close behind him. His immediate thought was that it was an intruder, so he braced himself, ready to face him. As he did so he also became aware of a sweet smell. Then, out of the corner of his eye, he saw that it was a ghostly woman. "I'm sure it was the ghost from the empty flat next door," he said. "Probably came through the wall for a bit of company. I turned to face her and she vanished. To be honest, I was relieved it was just her, and not the burglar I'd been expecting."

The neighbour also told me how, on the day that Greg and Emma left the flat for good, the ghost could be heard sobbing through the walls all night, and at two in the morning, took to throwing objects about. This behaviour would certainly account for the smashed plates on the kitchen floor and the broken radio which Clark had described.

COMING TO A SCREEN NEAR YOU

Today there are thousands of satellite, cable and terrestrial channels available that cater for the interests of most television viewers, but the more mature reader will recall the days when the UK only had BBC1, which first went on air in November 1936; ITV which was launched in September 1955, followed by BBC2, which began broadcasting in April 1964 and Channel 4 which was transmitted into our homes in November 1982.

In those days, the four television stations usually ceased their transmissions between midnight and 1am. For example, on the night of Thursday, 12 August 1982, BBC 1 went off air after the 12.05am weather forecast and BBC 2 closed down at the same time, after the highlights from the first day of the Second Test between England and Pakistan. Granada

Television ended its service at 12.45am, after *What the Papers Say* and a charity appeal programme called *Lifeline*. The television stations would go back on air in the morning between 6.30am and 9am, and during that off-air time, in the absence of any signals from the television transmitters, 'white noise' would be all that could be picked up on any television set that happened to be switched on.

In these days of perpetual television transmissions, it is rare to see the speckled pattern of white noise on our screens, unless you have a set that is disconnected from a terrestrial aerial cable, or unplugged from a cable or Satellite decoder.

On the date which I mentioned earlier - 12 August 1982 - a paranormal incident took place involving white noise that has never been satisfactorily explained. At her home in Halewood, thirty-nine-year-old Ruth Lorrey was sitting in her favourite armchair at 11.30pm on that Thursday night in August, idly watching the end credits of *Hill Street Blues* scroll up the screen. Ruth emitted a loud yawn and then sank into one of those surprisingly fulfilling armchair naps, that often seem to be more refreshing than an eight-hour stretch in a comfortable king-sized bed.

She awoke at five minutes to two in the morning to a harsh hissing noise, and for a moment she thought the shower had been left on full in the bathroom, before she realised that it was coming from the television. She rose from the armchair with a stiff neck, and was shuffling across the carpet to switch off the television, when she suddenly noticed something rather odd. Within the static snow on the television screen, there was a faint silhouetted figure - and it was stepping towards her. The figure was plainly male and, as far as she could make out, had short-hair and was clean cut, as if wearing a suit.

When the silhouette came close enough to fill the whole screen with just its head and shoulders, it suddenly veered off towards the right, disappearing from view. Simultaneously, a distinct draught of cold air passed Ruth on her right. A crackling sound - similar to the discharge of static electricity you sometimes hear when a comb is dragged through long dry hair - was also heard along the wall to her right. An earthenware ornament of a hedgehog that Ruth's niece had bought her as a birthday gift, then slid along a shelf as the crackling cold 'presence' passed by, leaving the distinctive fresh smell of ozone in its wake. She clearly recalled that tingly aroma of ionised air from a childhood summer's day on the sands at New Brighton, when the Tower Ballroom was struck by a bolt of lightning.

Ruth quickly switched off the television and sat pondering on what had just taken place. She wondered if the image of the approaching man on the screen had been merely some late-night film showing on another channel, that had somehow overlapped on to the Granada channel. To test this theory, she switched the television back on and pressed each of the channel buttons in turn, but found that every station was off air.

Feeling more than a little spooked, and knowing that she would not sleep if she went straight to bed, she then switched the television off and turned on the radio instead for company. Her husband had separated from her almost a year ago, and her fifteen-year-old daughter Hannah was staying over at her friend's house in Gateacre. Ruth realigned the pottery hedgehog on the shelf, then went to make herself a coffee in an effort to steady her frayed nerves.

Almost a fortnight later, Hannah invited two of her schoolmates, Donna and Sheree, to her home for a stay-over. Ruth went to bed at around 10pm to get out of the girls' way. The trio watched a late-night horror movie, and when the film ended, sometime after 1am, the girls swapped ghost stories. At around 2am, Sheree said to Hannah, "Hey! Switch the telly on. You might see the shadow man."

Hannah asked who the Shadow Man was. Sheree was something of a joker, but was unusually serious, for once. She said she had heard there was a weird man who came out of television sets that were left on at night. Her aunt in Huyton had seen him, and so had lots of other people.

"You're a liar," snapped Donna. "What a load of old rubbish," and there was almost a fight. Hannah switched on the television to diffuse the situation, but there was only the usual static blizzard and loud roaring noise, so she turned down the volume. Sheree was eager to see if what her aunt had told her was true and she encouraged her mates to sit down and watch the screen. "If you stare at the screen long enough, he'll come," she promised.

Donna giggled and switched off the living-room lights. The three girls sat in a row on the carpet, watching the dancing spots on the face of the cathode ray tube. "Who is he, anyway?" Hannah wanted to know.

"I don't know," admitted Sheree, "but my aunt said

he comes to her in the night sometimes, when she leaves the telly on at all hours in the morning."

A split-second after Sheree had uttered that sentence, a dim dark "wriggling" spot appeared in the centre of the screen. The girls watched, motionless. The nervous tension hanging in the air thick enough to cut with a knife.

"What's that thing?" Hannah asked, wide-eyed. She didn't like this thing one little bit.

The spot gradually expanded until it formed the grey silhouette of a man who was walking towards the screen. He was just a few inches tall at first, but as he drew nearer and nearer, his height increased. The girls quickly scrambled up from their sitting positions and backed away from the television. Fully expecting the figure to jump out of the screen at any moment, they ran out of the house and made their way to Sheree's home in Manor Road, Woolton. When Ruth awoke on the following morning, she went into her daughter's bedroom and discovered that her bed had not been slept in. She searched everywhere in the house and discovered that Hannah and her friends were nowhere to be found. She telephoned Donna's house and there was no answer, so she rang Sheree's parents, and was greatly relieved when her mother said they were all fine and were having breakfast together, laughing and joking. When Hannah later told her mother about the 'Shadow Man' who came out of the television, Ruth shuddered. She instantly recalled the paranormal figure who had emerged from the set almost two weeks ago. Ruth got in touch with Sheree's aunt, a woman named Esther, and asked her about her experiences with the Shadow Man. Esther was a little reluctant at first to talk about the supernatural incidents she had witnessed to a perfect stranger, but when Ruth told her about her own experience and the thing that Hannah, Donna and Sheree had seen, she opened up.

Esther said that on four occasions she had not only seen a shadowy figure appear on the screen, long after all programmes after closedown; she had also, on two occasions, seen a shadowy figure walk through her living-room. Both times the figure had been made up of thousands of tiny flickering spots. These manifestations had happened minutes after Esther had seen the silhouetted figure of a man on her television screen.

Esther had first discovered that the television was not normal when she had inadvertently left it on one night, as she was doing the washing up. The figure always put in an appearance when there was a sea of static on the screen. She had mentioned it to her friend Barbara, who lives in Widnes, and was amazed to find that she too had seen the same ghostly images on her television screen after the programmes had closed down.

I have since collected many reports of the alleged phantoms of the white noise, and the earliest account I have dates back to July 1978, when an elderly couple in Fazakerley saw a man's smiling face on their television screen for three nights in a row, even though their old set was switched off. That report, however, did not involve white noise.

The most recent white noise-related 'ghost' was reported in October 2008, from a young woman living in Calderstones. She was dozing in bed late one night, watching a film on her DVD player. Shortly after the film ended, the DVD player was left on for some time, then automatically shut off, leaving the screen without any signal, because it was not connected to any terrestrial, cable or satellite channels. Deep in thought, the girl looked at the snowy screen, full of white noise, for a few moments, then nearly shot out of bed when she saw a little silhouetted man walking towards her on the screen. He got bigger and bigger then veered off to the right, disappearing off-screen.

The girl was so unnerved by the figure, that she shouted for her boyfriend. He said the telly was probably just picking up transmissions from the transmitter of some other channel, and to try and prove his theory, he sat watching the white noise on the screen for some time. No more images were visible, and thankfully, the sinister Shadow Man has not put in an appearance since.

The nature of the phantoms of the white noise is difficult to fathom, but white noise has controversially supplied researchers into the paranormal with so-called EVP - Electronic Voice Phenomenon - which consists of audio messages, most of them cryptic, that are captured whenever white noise is recorded (whether on tape, CD, or in MP3 format) and later played back. It would seem that the circuits of the domestic television can do more than pick up and decode broadcast signals from afar. It is possible, under certain circumstances, that the cathode ray tube, and its modern counterpart, the plasma screen, can open up an electronic portal to some other plane of existence.

Unless you would like to personally investigate the Shadow Man, I would advise you, in the unlikely event of a cable or satellite channel going off air at night, to switch off your television set, or, as the old television continuity announcers once used to tell viewers at closedown: "A very good night to you. Sleep well, and please don't forget to switch off your set."

NO PLACE LIKE A HAUNTED HOME

It would seem that most people, after they have died, either enter a period of rest - a hibernatory hiatus - whilst in the spirit state, or, they 'pass over' to the life beyond, usually after a period of three days. A small percentage of the deceased 'stay on' for a while - sometimes for quite a while - haunting their former home or workplace. A case in point took place at a house on Marmion Road, Aigburth.

For many years, through the late Victorian era, the Edwardian period, and for a greater part of the twentieth century, the ghost of an elderly woman manifested itself at this address. The ghost is believed to be that of Abigail Isaac, a Jewish woman who died at the house in May 1899, aged seventy-eight. She was buried at the Jewish cemetery in Deane Road, but not long afterwards, old Abigail was seen on many occasions back at her home on Marmion Road, walking upstairs and popping into the nursery room, and talking to a child.

This ghost periodically makes itself scarce for a while, sometimes for years at a time, before returning to haunt the rooms of its old home. The house in question is, at the time of writing, sub-divided into four flats, but the partitions and brick-and-mortar dividers are of no significance to the ghost of Mrs Isaac, which passes through walls with the ease of a hand passing through a beam of light.

A few years ago, a couple living on the first floor of the haunted Aigburth house began to hear dull, but distinctive, footsteps on the stairs, at all hours in the morning. The woman was afraid of the sounds at first, fearing that burglars had gained access to the house, but when the nocturnal pacing had gone on for a few nights, her fear turned to curiosity one night, when she heard the footsteps stop outside their door, and she quickly opened it to find no one there.

Another couple, upstairs, heard voices in their three-year-old daughter's bedroom one night and rushed in to find an old, quaintly-dressed woman with a wizened face and a toothless, sucked-in mouth, leaning over the child's bed, whispering something. The little girl shrank back in fear, and as the old woman vanished, her parents picked her up and took her into their room. I am not sure if the ghost still haunts the Marmion Road flats in the twenty-first century, but I would not be at all surprised if it did, as this type of haunting often continue for centuries.

Two other ghosts who frequently return from beyond the grave to visit their former home are heard, more than they are seen. One of these ghosts is that of a woman, who, according to the various sightings, seems to be about fifty years of age. The second is that of a man, who may be her brother, and looks as if he is in his late thirties, or early forties. The house where the duo appear is in Fairburn Road, Tuebrook, one of the eight parallel streets that end in 'burn' off Lisburn Lane. 'Burn' is an old northern England and Scottish word for a stream or brook, and refers to the stream from which Tuebrook derived its name. Incidentally, the brook which still runs under Tuebrook was named after the Norse god Tiu.

The underground stream runs from Green Lane, beneath Lisburn Lane, and on into Clubmoor, where it continues through to Walton Hall Park, Evered Avenue, Rice Lane Recreation Ground, Hartley's Village, Long Lane, until finally, at the junction of Hazel Grove, the stream becomes Fazakerley Brook, which ultimately runs into the coast-bound River Alt.

Over the years, researchers into the paranormal have discovered that places where water is running, whether in a river, or subterranean stream, seem to have a high incidence of psychic phenomena. This is certainly the case in Tuebrook, which is one of the most haunted districts of Liverpool. Most of the ghosts of Tuebrook seem to haunt locations that are situated above the underground stream. A phantom woman in a hooded cloak haunts Green Lane, and Malvern House, in particular, and there are other hauntings that coincide with the path of the Tiu Brook, including the following, on Fairburn Road.

THE ODD COUPLE

The little terraced redbrick house on Fairburn Road seemed welcoming enough when fifty-five-year-old widow, Irene, and her thirty-four-year-old son Malcolm moved into it, in the 1980s, but they soon discovered that the dwelling had a supernatural reputation. A week after Irene moved into the house, a female neighbour asked her if she had "seen anything" in the living room. Irene was puzzled by this question, and when she asked for an explanation, the woman just said, "Oh, nothing," and changed the subject.

About three days later, Malcolm rushed into the kitchen as his mother was making the tea and gasped, "Mum, some people are in there!"

His mother carried on stirring the gravy to go with the bangers and mash she was preparing, and without showing any interest asked, "Who, love?"

"They're in the living room ... Come and have a look, if you don't believe me."

Malcolm took hold of his mother's elbow and gently

steered her away from the cooker. Irene allowed herself to be guided through the hallway, to the doorway to the living room. Sitting on the sofa, as large as life, was a woman dressed in what used to be called 'sensible' clothes: a chocolate brown cardigan, black knee-length skirt, tan stockings and buckled shoes. Her hair was red and curly, in no particular style, and perched on her nose was a pair of quaint horned-rim spectacles. Her age was difficult to gauge, but Irene judged her to be about fifty.

Sitting primly alongside her was a slightly younger man, of about forty, maybe. The only distinctive thing about him was his hair, which was short, black and oily and slicked over to one side from a severe parting. His pale blue long-sleeved shirt, sleeveless dark blue sweater, black trousers and black slip-on shoes were almost a uniform for a certain type of rather boring suburban male; probably a bank clerk, thought Irene, or one of those anonymous men who do the same office job all their lives.

This odd couple were staring blankly at the wall opposite, as they sat in silence on the sofa, and did not seem to be aware of Irene and Malcolm. Irene gave a little cough, but the strangers still did not react. Mother and son then backed away into the hallway and Malcolm closed the parlour door. He was far more unnerved by the eerie visitors than his mother. Irene was certainly not delighted that her living room had been invaded by what could only be two ghosts, yet she was also intrigued by their presence. Who were they and why were they here? Meanwhile, a white faced Malcolm had put on his overcoat, and announced that he was going to his Uncle Ray's. Irene persuaded him to stay a moment, whilst she reopened the parlour door. She fully expected the visitants to have gone, but they were still there, staring straight ahead, as still as statues.

Irene looked back at Malcolm, who returned an expression of pure fear. She then looked back into the parlour, and to her surprise and relief saw that the man and woman had vanished as mysteriously as they had appeared, leaving a sweet smell in their wake. "They're gone," she said, her voice barely a whisper.

"What?" Malcolm asked, but refused to come and see for himself. He also refused to stay in the house that night, and went, with his mother, to her brother Ray's home in Old Swan. They stayed overnight at Ray's house, and returned to the haunted house on Fairburn Road on the following day around noon. They were both apprehensive, but for almost a week they saw nothing of the ghosts. Then, on the sixth day, something terrifying took place at the house.

Malcolm was in the shower at around 7pm. He had put a portable radio on the bathroom window ledge for company, and its volume was turned up quite loud. Downstairs, Irene had just put her feet up in front of the television. Malcolm was singing along to a song blaring out from the radio, as he worked his hair up to a thick lather and the bathroom filled with steam.

All of a sudden, he felt something icy slithering over his collarbones. Despite the shampoo trickling into one eye, he could see a pair of withered claw-like fingers sliding down to the top of his chest. What sort of monstrosity was behind him in the cubicle? And what was it going to do to him? Without stopping to find out, he lunged sideways, pushed open the door and jumped out of the shower. With his slippery sud-coated hands he fumbled with the catch of the bathroom door, aware of the figure advancing behind him.

Somehow, he managed to escape from the bathroom and he ran, half-blinded by the shampoo, down the stairs, and into the parlour, where his mother was watching television. She gasped in surprise when a dripping wet Malcolm burst in, naked as the day he was born! Slamming the door shut behind him, he snatched an embroidered anti-macassar from an armchair and used it to wipe the shampoo from his eyes.

As Malcolm hurried into the kitchen to find a newly laundered bath towel, Irene went into the hall and listened at the bottom of the stairs. All she could hear was the hissing of the shower and the radio. She was just about to go and quiz Malcolm about his bizarre behaviour, when there came another sound - the sound of footsteps - faint at first, then getting louder as they came down the stairs. Irene was made of sterner stuff than her timid offspring, and she stood her ground and waited tensely for the impending confrontation. Nevertheless, an irritating dizziness came over her as the gentle thumps reached the bottom of the stairs and she heard someone walk past her and head into the living room, leaving behind a trail of wet footprints on the hall floor.

There was no further spooky activity that day, but Irene was now almost as spooked as her son. She felt as though her privacy had been invaded and her home violated and neither she nor Malcolm slept a wink that night with their frayed nerves.

About a week later, Malcolm woke up at 2.40am to go to the lavatory. On his way back, as he crossed the landing, he heard voices downstairs. He could hear his mother snoring softly in her bedroom, so he knew she was not downstairs and, besides, who would she be talking to at this late hour? He strained his ears to listen. He could not make out their conversation, but he was able to identify a male and a female voice. He crept down a few steps and, pressing his face to the banisters, he listened again. The door to the back parlour suddenly opened, making him nearly jump out of his skin. Loud laughter rang out.

By the light of the street lamp shining into the hallway, Malcolm could make out the same two staid looking figures he had seen weeks before sitting in the front parlour, only this time they were much more animated. The woman was laughing hysterically, but the younger man was shaking his head from side to side, as if he were suffering a fit ... and there was something in his mouth ... something live! Malcolm crouched down as far as he dared, without giving himself away, the better to focus on the truly surreal and sickening sight that was to follow.

Malcolm soon saw the source of the woman's mirth - the man had his teeth clenched around a live budgerigar's head, and its wings were fluttering wildly. Suddenly, he yanked the body away and then spat out the head, as if it were nothing more than an orange pip. He let go of the poor headless budgie and its body flew off a short distance and landed on the stairs, where it flapped in circles for a few moments, before falling still. Foam and blood was oozing out of the man's mouth and one or two brightly coloured feathers stuck to his lips.

The woman abruptly stopped laughing - not because the sick performance was finally over - but because she had spotted Malcolm squatting on the stairs and she pointed him out to the man with blood dribbling down his chin, who he flew up the stairs, taking them two at a time.

Malcolm bolted back to his bedroom, his heart pounding. He slammed the door shut and pressed his body against it, with his hand held tight on the doorhandle. In less than a second, that handle twisted round with a superhuman force, as if connected to the drive shaft of an engine, and an equally powerful force shoved the door open a few inches. Malcolm leaned at a forty-five-degree angle in a desperate effort to reclose it, but it only inched open even wider. He scanned the room for something with which to clobber the weird intruder, without fully acknowledging that there was a ghost on the other side of the door. Then his eyes fell on his electric guitar, propped up against the wall over in the corner, and he calculated that its solid heavy wooden body would inflict a fair amount of damage to the maniac's head. He knew it was gamble, but he could not keep the madman out any longer, so he let go of the door and dashed across the room to get the guitar. The door immediately flew open behind him - but there was nobody there. Malcolm was so terrified that he could not take in the fact that his pursuer had vanished, and he stood there brandishing the guitar for about fifteen minutes, before he dared set foot outside his bedroom. He checked his mother's room and found her fast asleep, then crept downstairs and turned on all the lights. There was no trace of the decapitated budgerigar on the stairs, nor was there any sign of the unearthly visitors. Finally, he woke his mother and told her what had happened, and then issued an ultimatum: "I'm leaving this house, Mum ... it's full of ghosts and if you don't come with me you'll have to live here alone."

Two days later, they moved in with Ray for a few weeks, until they found a little house in Bromborough, close to Irene's cousin June. The mother and son never moved back to that Tuebrook house, but later occupants have allegedly heard strange laughter in the dead of night, seen a shadowy figure run silently up and down the stairs, and heard a bird (perhaps that ill-fated budgerigar) flapping its wings in the hallway.

No one knows whose ghosts are haunting the house on Fairburn Road, but an elderly woman, who has sadly now passed away, once told me that they were an unsavoury brother and sister from the outskirts of Liverpool, or possibly St Helens. The only dealings the strange pair had with their neighbours were fuelled by hate. The sister had become bitter and twisted through her self-imposed isolation, and was known to send people in the area poison pen letters. The brother was equally anti-social and unpleasant, being a notorious peeping tom, who prowled the district after dark, often climbing into back yards and peering through people's windows. The reclusive brother and sister died in a car crash some time in the 1960s. Someone out there will undoubtedly will be able to throw more light on this sinister case.

HEAD CASE

I don't quite understand the mechanism by which it occurs, but sometimes the evil deeds committed in a house can somehow be perpetrated on the new occupants, years after they have taken place. In the summer of 2004, for example, Tony, a supermarket stock clerk, woke up one morning to a terrifying experience at his flat in Walton.

Tony's alarm clock began to bleep at 6.30am, and he tried to open his eyes but the lids felt like lead. He tried to lift his head off the pillow, but felt as if it were encased in concrete. His next instinct was to raise his hands to his head and find out what was covering it, but he could not do that either, because his arms - and also, he discovered - his legs, were bound to the bed. He tried to take a deep breath, because whatever his head was held in, it was barely letting in any air, but he could not and he panicked. He began to hyperventilate as he tried to suck in air through his paralysed mouth and strained in vain to open his eyes. The alarm clock continued to bleep, then gave up for a while, then bleeped again for a few minutes, then stopped dead. Hours seemed to pass and Tony's strange paralysis persisted. He tried to cry out for help but found he couldn't open his mouth wide enough.

Then, all of a sudden, the paralysis wore off and Tony was able to sit upright in bed, gasping for air. His arms were free and unrestrained and he looked at his pillow to see what strange device had entrapped his head - but there was nothing there except traces of sweat. The terrifying experience, which, it transpired, had lasted no more than five minutes, was dismissed as a nightmare, but on two more occasions, the alarming paralysis returned with the exact same 'symptoms'.

Tony ended up having a brain scan and other tests and a neurological problem was ruled out. The doctor believed the experiences had been caused by stress, which, in certain cases, can cause stiffening of the muscles of the head, neck and limbs, although Tony felt he had been fobbed off and that the real cause of his symptoms lay elsewhere. Shortly afterwards, he was offered another job with better pay and less stress at a supermarket in Cheshire, and he grabbed the opportunity with both hands. He moved from the flat on Walton Road to a house in Ellesmere Port, and after the move, the paralysis incidents ceased, so he assumed the doctor had been right after all, and he put the incidents behind him and got on with his life.

Then a chance meeting with the landlord of the Walton flat, at a cafe in Liverpool, threw some new and disturbing light on Tony's previous experiences. The landlord, an elderly man called Eric, gave Tony the details of a peculiar story.

Around 1980, a couple in their twenties had lived in the Walton flat that Tony had occupied. Their names were Jackie and Glenn. Jackie was a greetings card designer and part-time art student, and Glenn worked at home manufacturing items for a novelty shop. He made key-ring fobs, ornaments and paperweights from a substance similar to Lucite, which, once set, was as transparent as glass but much harder. Glenn's job was to suspend various items in this substance, and at that time, they were something of a craze, especially amongst young people, and sold quite well.

Glenn genuinely loved Jackie, but he was a very jealous man, and had, on several occasions, accused her of having an affair with a tutor at the art college. One day, this jealous streak of Glenn's proved too much for Jackie, and she deliberately stayed out drinking after college till late.

Glenn, of course, imagined she was seeing someone, and, on this occasion, he was right, because when she returned in the early hours, she told him to his face that she had been seeing Terry - her art teacher. This revelation enraged Glenn and provoked a string of abuse, but then he noticed that Jackie seemed to be taking pleasure in his wild reaction, so he forced himself to calm down and instead plotted what he saw as a sweet, but twisted, act of revenge, like something straight out of the books of Edgar Allan Poe. Glenn was an insomniac, and relied on sleeping pills to get to sleep. To set his plan in motion, he tipped four of these pills out of their bottle, opened up the capsules and poured the powder into a glass of vodka. He then pretended to make up with Jackie, whilst inwardly seething like a volcano about to erupt, and Jackie fell for it. She had already had a lot to drink that night, so when she drank the vodka she quickly fell into a dangerously deep sleep.

Whilst she was in this agitated state, Glenn carried her limp form to the table in his workroom and stretched her out on it. He stood for a few moments viewing with disgust her lolling head and slack mouth, and cheeks flushed with alcohol. The first stage of his elaborate plan involved shaving off Jackie's beautiful black curly hair with his electric hair clippers. This he did in the roughest and most careless way - he was punishing her, after all, he reasoned. By the time he had finished, her scalp was red raw and covered all over in nicks and cuts and small tufts of hair where he had missed a bit. He stood back and surveyed the result with satisfaction. "Don't think that Terry would fancy going on a date with you now, would he?" he smirked.

A trip to the kitchen saw him returning clutching a packet of multicoloured drinking straws. He removed a small bundle of the straws and stuffed some of them up her nose and a few others in her mouth. Next he cut out a U-shaped section from the side of a plastic casting box, which he used to make his ornaments and positioned Jackie's head inside it. He noted with satisfaction that her neck protruded perfectly through the U-shaped hole he had cut out of one side of the box, and he gave himself a mental pat on the back for his craftsmanship.

Now for the final act in his sick little drama. Taking

care not to spill any - this stuff cost money - he carefully poured the liquid chemical into the mould, until it was full to the brim. Jackie's head was now immersed in the Lucite-like liquid, which was as transparent as water. So deeply unconscious was she, that she didn't even flinch, and the straws ensured that she had just enough air to breathe. A few tiny bubbles came up from her mouth but the liquid had properties which did not allow these bubbles to become trapped in the moulding.

Glenn then sat in a corner to survey his handiwork, and it was then that the enormity of what he had just done slowly dawned on him. He started crying, not for Jackie, but for himself, because he knew he would probably be sectioned for what he had just done. He was about to try and lift Jackie's head out of the box of liquid glass before it hardened, but then he remembered what she had said about her and Terry, and he gritted his teeth and abandoned her to her fate. He left the flat and drove around for a while, wondering where he could hide. He thought of going on the run and hiding out in Wales, like an outlaw, but he couldn't come to any decision.

The hours ticked by and Glenn eventually drove back to his flat to find that the liquid had set like stone. Encased in a cube of transparent acrylic glass was the grotesque shaven head of his partner. He listened to the tips of the straws leading from her nostrils and mouth, and detected a faint hissing sound and her chest was rhythmically rising and falling. "What have I done?" Glenn asked himself, viewing the wreck of the once beautiful woman he loved. He knew that Jackie would start to panic the moment she woke up, and he could not allow her to get up with her head encased in that block - the weight of it could break her neck. So he cut the flexes off his television set and electric iron, and set about binding her wrists and ankles together, to stop her from moving. The old washing line in the back yard was cut down and used to tie the unconscious young woman to the work bench. Glenn then sat down to await developments.

When finally she awoke, almost ten hours later, an unimaginable terror must have overtaken the stricken woman. She couldn't even open her eyes, as the hard plastic had welded her eyelids shut. A series of violent spasms wracked her whole body, and the now loud hissing from the straws sent Glenn into a panic. He ran out of the flat, his mind in turmoil. What if she tried to throw up because of the previous night's drinking? She would choke on her own vomit and then he would be a murderer. The weight of the terrible thing he had done bore down on him, crushing him, until he could stand it no more and he confessed all to a policeman who happened to be passing.

Within the half hour, the girl was freed from the bench on which she had been tortured, and was rushed to the local hospital, but her troubles were still far from over. The doctors were faced with a terrible dilemma - if the block was struck too hard, her skull could be damaged and even if it were not, would the plastic tear off Jackie's face when it was removed? In the event, a surgeon used solvents and a flaw in the plastic block at the back of Jackie's head to remove the nightmarish encasement.

After her release, the girl hyperventilated and screamed inconsolably for a very long time, as the nurses and surgeons attempted to reassure her that her ordeal was now over. Then Jackie felt her bare scalp and realised that her lovely hair, her pride and joy, was gone. Yet if Glenn had not shaved off her hair, the removal of the plastic block would have been even more difficult and exceedingly painful.

Glenn was placed under psychiatric supervision, and Jackie went to live with her parents in Wirral for a year. She made a good physical recovery from her trauma under the care of her parents and eventually she felt well enough to brave the outside world again. Before long, she met someone else, married him, and went to live in France, but the abuse suffered at the hands of her deranged ex-partner Glenn must have haunted her for years, and probably continues to do so to this day. When Tony heard this story he shuddered. His late mother had always told him he was psychic, and now he finally accepted that she was right. He had somehow picked up some sort of impression of the terror left behind in that flat after the shocking torture of Jackie.

BEHIND THE GREEN DOOR

So much death and tragedy in the world has actually been perpetrated because of boredom. King Louis XIV of France and Navarre was prone to bouts of ennui, which prompted him to start wars that extinguished thousands of lives.

In November 1973, two bored National Airline pilots at the controls of a DC10 carrying one hundred and fifteen passengers, suddenly decided to meddle with the auto-throttle system - seemingly just for something to do. This was at an altitude of 39,000 feet, sixty-five miles southwest of Albuquerque, New Mexico. The fan assembly of jet-engine 3 disintegrated as a result of their little experiment, and the ensuing explosion ripped through the fuselage and broke one of the passenger windows.

The unfortunate passenger sitting in the seat next to this cabin window weighed two hundred pounds, and yet he was sucked through a window which only measured one foot by two feet. A handful of the braver passengers tried to cling on to his legs, but he was wrenched from their grip by the powerful outrush of pressurised air which sucked him to a terrifying death. His body was never recovered.

The plane made an emergency landing and twenty-four injured passengers received immediate medical treatment. All this took place because a flight engineer and a pilot were bored. Boredom has a lot to answer for, and it was this mental state that got two young Liverpool men into trouble one evening in the 1960s.

Harry Toby and Brian Dunne, both in their early twenties, were bored stiff; that particular type of Sunday boredom that used to characterise the day of rest for many young people craving a bit of excitement in their lives. It was a hot lazy August late evening in 1966, and Harry, who bore a strong resemblance to the singer (and later actor) Adam Faith, was vainly ogling himself in front of a full-length mirror in Brian's bedroom, trying out different poses. Brian was slouched on the floor in the corner, taking the occasional swig of cider from a bottle, as the portable record player crackled and then boomed out Chris Farlowe singing his hit single, *Out of Time*.

Moments later a muffled thud was heard from beneath the floor - Brian's mother was thumping the parlour ceiling with the shaft of a brush. In response, Brian turned the volume up even more. "You're obsolete, my baby ..." sang Harry at the top of his voice to his dancing mirror image. The tip of the brush shaft thudded repeatedly like a muffled machine gun, so with a huff, Brian finally turned the volume down and flopped down on the bed.

Harry sauntered over to the window and opened its S-shaped catch to let some air into the claustrophobic room and looked idly out into Grove Street. As usual on Sunday evenings, it was completely dead, not a soul about. The peel of church bells way off in the distance was temporarily drowned out by a bluebottle's monotonous drone. Harry swatted the fly with the back of his hand and it dropped like a stone on to the sill, where, after a few seconds of frenzied circling on its back, it recovered and flew lazily out of the window.

Presently, Brian hauled himself up off the bed and joined Harry at the window, jostling for elbow room, before lapsing into one of those vacant moods that can befall anyone who imbibes too much alcohol. The two young men looked across at the Liverpool skyline. The rooftops in the distance were hazed by Tyndall blue, and the sky had just lost the sun, yet there was still enough light reflecting from the sky's canopy, by which to see the street, but the temperature was dropping and darkness was slowly infiltrating the world in its usual insidious way at day's end.

Harry looked northwards, and frowned slightly as his attention became focused on a forgettable-looking terraced house further up Grove Street. The hedges were overgrown behind low, blackened sandstone walls, and lovestone ivy had obliterated most of the building's anaemic facade. The windows of this ghastly-looking frontage were misted over with years of grime - far more effective than net curtains in frustrating the curiosity of passers-by - and the door's faded green paint was flaking. The building was flanked by a derelict house on one side and an unoccupied house on the other. Harry had noticed before that this dismal dwelling seemed to be permanently shadow, whether viewed by day or by night. At this moment, it lay just outside the rays of a feeble street lamp which had just come on further down the road.

"Who lives in that scruffy house over there?" Harry asked, pointing it out.

"Oh, that dump! Yeah, it's haunted."

"What? With ghosts and that?" laughed Harry, with a sarcastic sidelong sneer.

"Well you can't have a haunted house without ghosts, can you?" quipped Brian.

"And who told you it was haunted?" Harry wanted to know. He didn't believe in ghosts.

"My mum and dad told me," said Brian, and he blushed for some reason and tried to hide it by turning his face away.

"Hey! You've gone all red," said, Harry, never one to miss a trick, and revelling in his friend's embarrassment.

Just then the bedroom door opened, and Brian's mother popped her head round. "Keep those records low, will you, lads? Your dad's asleep in the chair, Brian, and he has to go to work at nine."

Mrs Dunne cast a disapproving eye over the three empty brown cider bottles lying next to the record player and shot her son an angry look. She tutted and was about to go when Harry called her back.

"Hey, Mrs Dunne, Brian was just telling me about the haunted house over there. Is it true, like?" and he nodded towards the open window.

"The one by Mrs Kenny's?" asked Mrs Dunne, ready to embark on one of her blow-by-blow accounts of the banshee she saw when she was a child.

"No, not that one, Mam ..." Brian interrupted, "... the other end of 'Grovey' [Grove Street] ... up that way," he pointed north, "... the house with the green door."

The reference to the house with the green door seemed to have a profound effect on Mrs Dunne, who stood tight-lipped for a moment or two. Finally, in a serious tone, she said, "Oh, I know the one you mean ... the place with all the ivy and the paint peeling off ... the one with the green door."

"That's a song, isn't it?" Harry whispered to his friend with a giggle, but Brian was not listening. He was gaping at his mother.

"Your dad tried to rob the lead off the roof of that house about ten years back ..." Mrs Dunne continued.

Harry quickly made the connection, realising why Brian had been embarrassed before at the mention of the house.

"He wasn't trying to rob it, Mam. He thought it was okay to take it because the place was empty," said a red-faced Brian, trying to put a better gloss on the bald fact that his father was a thief. He shot an anxious glance at Harry, who was pretending to scratch his nose to hide a smirk.

"Oh, Harry probably already knows all about your dad," said Mrs Dunne, who did not seem to share her son's embarrassment, and she smiled at Harry and continued with her story unabashed.

"Mum!" cried Brian, cringing with shame, "Will you please shut up? Harry doesn't want to listen to all this."

But Harry just patted his back in a reassuring way and said, "Shush! Listen to what she's got to say, Bri."

Mrs Dunne needed no further invitation and came into the room and sat herself down on the edge of the bed, ready to spill the beans. Brian's humiliation was now complete and he resigned himself to the months of mockery that would follow, once she had revealed all the family's shameful secrets. Mindless of her son's feelings, she began to relate a very strange tale.

Mrs Dunne's husband Hughie was aware that the keys to his house conveniently fitted the locks of many other houses on Grove Street, perhaps because the landlord, who owned much of the street, had used cheap locks on some of his premises. In particular, Hughie had found, to his initial delight, that the key to his home fitted the lock of the empty-looking house with the green door. He had had his eye on the property for some time, hoping to rob the lead from the roof and also remove any other scrap, such as the copper boiler tank.

And so it was, that at three o'clock one morning, Hughie turned the key in the dilapidated green door and ventured inside. The door creaked loudly, as it obviously had not been opened in years, but the vestibule door was wide open and Hughie found a huge pile of envelopes on the floor there. Most of these were addressed to a Mrs V Fisher, and the postmark on one of these letters dated it to 1938. Hughie stuffed the most promising-looking of these letters into his pocket, before exploring the front parlour.

He pushed the parlour door open slightly and noted that the room was still furnished, but a thick layer of dust covered everything like a ghostly shroud. He opened the drawers of a sideboard and was disappointed to find them empty, except for the translucent skins that woodworm larvae had shed over the years. Next, Hughie turned his attention to the back parlour, or dining room, and before he even opened the door, he heard a baby crying. He opened the door a crack and recoiled. A long dining table was being used as some kind of altar. It was covered with burning candles and amongst the expensive-looking tableware there was a live baby, kicking on its back on an oval silver platter.

Hughie's first natural instinct was to rescue the poor child, but then his eyes became more accustomed to the darkness within the room, and he could make out some grotesque-looking faces beyond the flickering glare of the candles. He shone his torch at one of these people and illuminated a sinister figure with an excessively high forehead and a black Van Dyke beard. He wore a black polo neck sweater. Hughie fled at that point, so afterwards he could not be absolutely sure if there had been a woman sitting next to this bearded man, or not.

Self preservation kicked in and Hughie flew out of the front door, leaving it wide open, and ran as fast as he could back to his home. He believed he heard people running behind him, but when he got to his own front door and looked back, he saw that Grove Street was completely empty and as silent as the grave. He woke his wife and told her what he had seen, and she told him to go to the police immediately, which he did.

In order to save his own skin, Hughie had to tell the

police that he had been drunk and had mistaken the house with the green door for his own house - even though his own house had a black front door! By sheer coincidence, his key had fitted the lock, and he had wandered in and witnessed what seemed to have been the start of some horrific cannibal feast. The police took his report seriously and inspected the house. They found the front door still ajar, but did not find any evidence of a baby on a silver plate. They did, however, find a dining room, but the candles which littered it were heavily cobwebbed, and the only footprints on the dusty floor were Hughie's own. The police cautioned Hughie and said he would be charged with wasting police time if he ever made such ridiculous and disturbing claims again. The story shocked Harry, and although Brian had heard it from his parents before, this time it began to play on his mind. He began to wonder if what his father had seen was the ghostly re-enactment of some cult that had practised cannibalism in that house many years ago.

At 10pm that night, after Brian's mother had left them alone, Harry put forward a rather scary proposition to his mate, "Look, we've been saying all evening how bored we are, so how about us going and taking a look at that house later?" His face was a picture of warped glee.

"Nah, you must be joking. Wild horses wouldn't pull me into that place," said Brian, shaking his Beatle-styled mop of dark-brown hair. "We might be bored, but we don't have to go looking for trouble."

However, Harry could be very persuasive, and eventually talked his friend into visiting the so-called haunted house a few days later. Brian found his copy of the old door key to his home, as the lock had been changed a year ago, and at half past one, on the Wednesday morning of 31 August 1966, the two young men set out for the ivy covered house at the end of Grove Street. They were about halfway to their destination, when a dog howled somewhere in the distance. Brian halted when he heard the unearthly howl. In his heightened state of anxiety it sounded like a werewolf, but Harry reasoned that "the stupid mutt" was probably just baying at the full moon, which was hanging low over the rooftops of Toxteth that night.

At last they reached the worn stone steps of the house. An odour of sweet decay surrounded the wan-coloured building; the same kind of odour that can often be detected in the grounds of a cemetery. Harry was not a psychic sensitive by any stretch of the imagination, and yet he felt as if the gloomy house was radiating tragedy. Scratched into the green door was the ubiquitous graffiti character of 'Chad', looking over his wall, as usual.

Brian fumbled for some time with the key in the rusty lock, and finally succeeded in opening the door, although he would have been happier if he had not; he had only agreed to come along to avoid his friend's ridicule. The door creaked open just the way it had ten years ago, when Mr Dunne senior had ventured inside.

"After you," said Brian, inviting Harry to make the first move, and his friend cautiously stepped inside the pitch black hallway. Brian clicked on the torch and its narrow beam threw a pale disc of light on to the opposite wall. Staying close together, they crept into the parlour and both took a sharp intake of breath as the torch beam highlighted the imprints of many boot soles in the thick stratum of dust on the floor. Maybe they were just the footprints of the police, who were alerted to the shocking goings on at the house a decade before, but they both secretly thought they looked much fresher than that.

The two urban explorers moved silently back into the hallway and hesitated at the door that must lead to the notorious dining room. Harry's unsteady hand reached out to the handle and twisted it firmly to the right. On this occasion there were no candles illuminating the parlour, but a shaft of silver moonlight was blazing through a gap in the half-opened plum-coloured velvet drapes. The table had been set by someone a long long time ago, with tall crystal glasses of long evaporated wine, now thickly coated with dust, and laced by the handiwork of generations of spiders. A thought immediately entered Harry's mind when he surveyed the silver cutlery and expensive-looking plates and other tableware; why hadn't anyone broken in here and taken those items? Had something scared them off, just like Brian's father?

The torch which had been illuminating the back parlour suddenly flitted out of the room, and the sound of heavy running footsteps could be heard running down the hallway. Harry spun round to see why his friend had chickened out. He went to run after him, but when he got to the doorway of the back parlour, he found his way barred by an obese woman in a long black ankle-length dress. Her face looked shiny and false, like that of a porcelain doll, and her hair was pulled up into a tight little bun, which looked ridiculous on the top of such a huge head and body.

Her sudden appearance sent a tingling shockwave

through Harry's whole body. He gulped, then slowly backed away towards the table. Something scuttled haphazardly across the floor, kicking up little puffs of dust in the moonlight. It sounded like the patter of a small dog, but when Harry looked down he saw that it had wide furry stripes and eight legs. It was an enormous hairy spider, with a globular abdomen as large and round as a ripe grapefruit. The sight of the over-sized arachnid filled him with such terror and revulsion that he lost control of his bladder. At the same time as the urine trickled in a hot stream down his legs, he felt the mouthparts of the beastly creature prodding at his ankles.

"She won't harm you unless I tell her to," wheezed the surprisingly well-spoken woman, hobbling her great bulk forwards, revealing a grotesque deformed face in the moonlight. One eye was much lower than the other and that displaced eye had no sclera - no white of the eye - but instead a dark substance which surrounded a yellowish iris. As she smiled she revealed a set of decayed yellow and misshapen teeth.

Harry cried out as he felt a sharp pain in his Achilles tendon. The spider had bitten him right through his trousers and his socks.

"Get away! Go on! Shoo!" shouted the woman at the overgrown spider, as if it were nothing more threatening than a friendly lap dog, wanting to give someone a lick, and it made its way, in a series of staccato jerks, across the dusty floor, before vanishing into a dark hole in a thick network of cobwebs in the disused fireplace. There were footsteps now in the hallway ... someone was coming down the stairs ... and the sound made Harry leap into action. He grabbed one of the heavy solid silver candlesticks from the table and without thinking, he struck the woman with the deformed pale face as hard as he could. He must have hit her very hard because blood sprayed out and small fragments of smashed yellow teeth flew everywhere. The woman screamed and held a pair of chubby hands to her face, as she stumbled backwards with blood dripping down her double-chins.

Harry seized his chance and ran past her into the hallway, noticing for the first time that his right foot and ankle were becoming numb and stiff. As he rushed towards the front door, which had been left open by Brian after his sudden desertion, a long arm reached over the banisters and tried to grab at his head, and succeeded in wrenching out a lock of the young man's hair and tearing it from his scalp. Harry yelled out in pain and stole a look at his assailant - a man dressed all in black, with a deathly pale face and a Van Dyke beard, glaring at him from the bottom of the stairs. He could also hear the eight-legged abomination scurrying after him down the hallway, and as soon as he reached the front door he slammed it shut behind him and staggered away, now barely able to walk with the pain. About a hundred feet away he came upon a rather shamefaced Brian standing in the moonlit street, the torch in his hand still switched on. He apologised for running off, but the sight of the weird-looking woman had put the wind up him. Harry could now no longer walk because his ankle had become so painful and swollen from the arachnid's bite. He told Brian about that giant spider, but his friend thought he was making it up - until Harry removed his shoe and sock when they got back to his house. His ankle was completely spherical and red raw. Two holes in the swelling were ringed by a yellow pus-like substance. Brian took one look at it, then used the family phone and dialled 999.

The ambulance was there within minutes, and Harry was taken to the Royal Hospital, on Pembroke Place. The doctors at the hospital could not agree on the cause of the extensive swelling. One physician thought it was the result of an allergic reaction from an insect bite, whereas another said the symptoms pointed to a rare type of gout. Harry, however, knew different.

For four agonising days, pus oozed out of the puncture marks in the strange wound and Harry shivered from a painful fever. It took almost a month for the swelling to subside and the stiffness to completely disappear from Harry's ankle. Harry used that month to reflect on his almost unbelievable experience, and decided that, in future, he would not allow his curiosity to lead him into any more potentially dangerous situations. He and Brian never set foot in that house on Grove Street again. Whatever mysteries were harboured within those walls, would have to remain mysteries, as far as they were concerned.

Two years after the terrifying incident, in 1968, Harry and Brian were drinking in a public house on Edge Lane called the Dryden, when they overheard an elderly man talking about the very house on Grove Street where they had encountered the two sinister figures and the overgrown spider. He was telling someone that his friend had been living as a vagrant, and had gained entry to the empty-looking house with a key one night during a heavy downpour. He had settled down to sleep under some old newspapers in the front parlour, but was awakened in the early hours of the morning by a peculiar looking couple, who angrily claimed that it was their house and he was trespassing.

As a punishment, the man held a long-bladed knife to the tramp's ear and then instructed him to kneel down in front of the enormously fat and disfigured-looking woman. She then lifted her skirts to reveal an abnormally bloated and grossly ulcerated leg. The tramp was then ordered, at knife point, to suck out the vile yellow substance that was oozing out of a running sore in the shin area of the woman's leg. He took one look at the pus-encrusted sore and was immediately overcome with nausea and he refused to do as he was bid.

The vagrant's refusal infuriated his persecutor and he thrust the blade tip forward slightly, piercing his eardrum. His head seemed to explode with pain, but now he knew that he had to comply with his revolting order, or die. And so he steeled himself to suck at the leg sore, desperately trying to fight back the waves of nausea and revulsion, which threatened to make him throw up all over the woman's shoes. Who knows what might have happened had he done so?

The filthy task completed, the couple let the tramp go and he stumbled his way straight to A and E. He was admitted to hospital and a stomach pump administered. Traces of an unknown toxin were drawn from his stomach. The police checked out his outlandish story, but found no evidence of anyone having lived in the house in question on Grove Street in recent years. The vagrant died a year later from chronic alcoholism.

The history of the house has been thoroughly researched, but no trace of a Mrs V Fisher can be found to corroborate the story. A ghost researcher once told me that the house was neither haunted by overgrown spiders, nor was it inhabited by weird couples who devoured babies, but rather a malevolent force - perhaps a demon - which played on the phobias and subconscious fears of those who entered the premises uninvited. It was certainly true that Harry Toby had always had a terrible fear of arachnids, and the vagrant who entered the house for shelter was himself suffering from an ulcerated leg at the time, so there may be some truth in this theory.

The house has long since been demolished and so now we may never learn the truth about the mysterious events that once went on behind that dilapidated green door ...

MR STRANKS

I was first told about the sinister Mr Stranks when I was a child, after I had come upon a drunken woman in tears one evening, lying prostrate over a grid in the roadway alongside a sprawling tenement block in Edge Hill. Apparently, the woman's young son had been run over many years before, and his crushed body had lain on that grid with his life blood oozing down that drain. The poor woman had never got over her child's tragic death, which she had witnessed at first hand. Some say the child had been hanging on to the back of an ice cream van just before the accident happened, when he lost his grip and fell into the road. A vehicle following close behind had no time to stop and ran right over the child, killing him outright. The ice cream van from which the child had slipped, was said to have been driven by a Mr Stranks.

My mother and another lady started talking about this weird Mr Stranks, an ice cream vendor who was seen all over Liverpool, but always at twilight, or during the hours of darkness. He travelled in what was possibly a Bedford CA 1968 van, but instead of the lively blue and cream, or red and white livery found on a normal ice cream van, Mr Stranks' van was painted a sombre dark green and black, more like a hearse.

The jingle of his gloomy-looking vehicle was neither the ubiquitous *Greensleeves*, nor *Popeye the Sailor Man*; tunes which are often chosen because they appeal to children. Instead, Mr Stranks chose a creepy tune which remained unidentified for many years, when I discovered that it was *Old Waits Carol*. The lyrics of this morbid sixteenth century song go like this:

The life of man is but a span,
And cut down in its flower,
We're here today, tomorrow gone,
The creatures of an hour.
Today you are alive and well,
Worth many a thousand pound.
Tomorrow dead, and cold as clay,
Your corpse laid underground.

So who exactly was this Mr Stranks? and what did he look like? Well, I threw this question open to listeners of a radio show I put out some years ago, and received back claims that he was a dangerous psychiatric patient, who had been released from a certain mental hospital after a large sum of money had changed hands. His father had allegedly promised the hospital's administrator that he would immediately take his insane son abroad and that no one would ever hear from him again, if he was granted his release. However, Mr Stranks senior died shortly afterwards and before he could fulfil his promise regarding his son.

Despite his poor mental state, Stranks inherited his father's wealth and lost no time in putting it to use for his own sinister ends. One person I interviewed - a woman named Teresa - maintained that Stranks was still at large as late as 1989, and still driving his distinctive gothic-looking ice cream van. She described him as a man with a head of thick curly brown hair, flecked with grey, and with a very pronounced Roman nose and a pair of abnormally large bulging eyes. I had an artist draw up Teresa's description of him and the final result, which she agreed was a pretty accurate representation, looked remarkably like the late comedian Marty Feldman.

Teresa had found her eight-year-old son crying near the black and green van one evening near her Huyton home. She had thought he was being looked after by his older sister, and was shocked to find him out on the street by himself at 10.30pm. The child had sneaked out as his sister was watching television, after hearing the ice cream van's chimes. The boy complained that the ice cream man had deliberately dropped his ice cream on the ground as he was handing it to him, and had then laughed and pulled faces at him.

That night, at around 11.15pm, the strange ice cream van was seen and heard on Rupert Road, disturbing the slumbers of local residents. Teresa and several other people noticed the words 'Mr Stranks' painted across a lamp on the front of the van, which then sped off towards Huyton Lane.

The earlier sightings of this van, if they are to be believed, date back to 1968, when the vehicle and its strange driver were seen regularly on Shaw Street, close to the Whitley Gardens play area during early dusk. There was an alleged report of a child being yanked into the van one evening and who knows what his fate might have been, had it not been for his quick-thinking sister, who managed to pull him back out of the vehicle to safety.

The green and black van made its next appearance near Newsham Park, on Strawberry Road, Norris Green, this time displaying a black skull and crossbones on its side. It was also seen driving after two children, as if trying to run them down, outside St Gabriel's Children's Home, on Beaconsfield Road, Woolton, and weeks later the ice cream van was heard at one o'clock in the morning on Gorsey Lane, Ford, close to the Tailor's Arms pub.

A Mr Briscoe, who, as a child, actually tasted the ice cream that Mr Stranks sold, said it was not at all like the popular Lyons-Maid, Saints, or Pendletons brands, but was rather soggy and tasteless. He had taken just one lick and then complained to Mr Stranks, upon which the ice cream man shook his fist at him and threatened that Briscoe's mother would drop dead. Dropping his ice cream, he ran off and fetched his father, but the van had disappeared by the time they returned to Gorsey Lane.

The people of Old Swan could barely believe their ears when, at three o'clock one morning, in December 1969, they were rudely awakened by the jangling amplified glockenspiel music of an ice cream van somewhere in their area. Who else would try and sell ice cream in the middle of the night but Mr Stranks? The police allegedly gave chase, but he went to ground and was never caught.

In 1971, a rumour spread that Mr Stranks had died in a crash. This was apparently backed up by a press report and the authorities at the time, but months later, the eerie ding-dong music of Old Waits Carol was heard once again somewhere in West Derby, by Yewtree Cemetery, on Finch Lane. This was at nearly four o'clock in the morning. A Mr Rotherham, who was on his way to work at a dairy at that ungodly hour, saw an ice cream van parked without any lights by the lodge house at the gates to the cemetery, and wondered why on earth it was playing its music when their were no people about, let alone children. By the meagre light of the full moon, Rotherham thought he could see a silhouetted figure creeping about inside the van and had the unsettling feeling that he was spying on him.

Other people I have talked to believe that Mr Stranks and his ice cream van were some sort of omen of death, or bad luck. There is no way of knowing whether this is true, unless more evidence comes to light. The people I spoke to were certainly convinced that he was real and a very unpleasant character, to boot. In the meantime, I will leave you with the last verse of the melancholy jingle which was played by Mr

THE PELLEW STREET HORROR

Stranks's ice cream van:

My song is done, I must be gone,
I can stay no longer here.
God bless you all, both great and small,
And send you a joyful new year.

THE VISITOR

It was half-past midnight on Wednesday, 14 July, 1965, when the following strange but true story began to unfold. A full moon was hanging brightly over West Derby, and two 13-year-old schoolboys had been allowed to camp out in a back garden to survey the splendour of the heavens with a new telescope. Barry was the owner of the brand new tripod-mounted telescope from Hobbies, and it was in the back garden of his friend Paul on Deysbrook Lane when the UFO was first seen. Barry had taken off his spectacles and squinted at the eyepiece of the telescope to scan the skies for Saturn – a big mistake with so much light from the full moon blotting out the minor stars. But then, at 1.20am, Paul happened to look directly overhead – and saw that something terrifyingly huge and circular was blocking out the stars and moonlight was glinting off its hull. The boys had recently been on a school trip to London and later, when describing the giant UFO to their bemused parents, Barry estimated that the diameter of the unknown craft had been about the same as the dome of St Paul's Cathedral (112 feet). Paul had tried to focus the telescope on the giant "flying saucer" but only momentarily saw its moonlit curvature. 'It was a cloud you saw,' Paul's father maintained. 'You saw a mirage of the moon, reflected off ice crystals in the atmosphere,' was the theory of Barry's dad, but three days later on Saturday 17th July, the colossal visitor returned to the skies of West Derby in the middle of the afternoon around 3.10pm. A roofer named Glyn was putting new slates on a friend's house in Mab Lane when he saw the massive steely saucer peeping from low clouds in the direction of West Derby Golf Course. Glyn and dozens of other people saw the silent invader of our airspace glide overhead, and one of these observers was the schoolboy Barry who had first seen the monster-size UFO three days back. The boy ran into his house, found an old Kodak camera, and took a few photographs of the ominous disc, which had a row of holes around its rim. Then it seemed to vanish. Barry pestered his father to have the film in the camera developed, and when the prints and negatives came back from the chemist days later, they showed scenes of last month's holiday in Wales – as well as a clear picture of the gargantuan UFO! 'On Monday morning we'll take it to the *Liverpool Echo* and get it printed,' Barry's dad promised, but something quite sinister took place that weekend. Sunday morning around 3am, Barry awoke and saw a beam of blue-green light "as thick as a candle" shining down into his room from something in the sky outside. Barry could hear his comics rustling about and his telescope being knocked over – apparently by this beam. He ran to his parents' room and when they returned with him they saw the toppled telescope and tripod – and comics scattered everywhere. That photograph of the UFO and its negative were never found. At present estimates the universe is 45 billion light years across with 100 billion galaxies that each contain hundreds of billions of stars with planets going round them – and our earth is just one of these planets. There are billions of earth-type worlds. To think we are alone in this universe is madness.

THE TAKERS

Now and then a sceptic will approach me, or drop me a line by snail-mail or email, to say that he or she found a certain story of mine unbelievable. My response is always the same - I tell them that I merely relay even the strangest stories from the public to my readers and leave it to them to make up their own minds. One foggy afternoon, a few years back, I was standing in St James's Cemetery, the vast sunken churchyard that lies next to the Anglican Cathedral, looking for a particular gravestone inscription as part of my research, when along came a man and his female friend, walking a dog. The couple were just passing me by, when the woman recognised me and muttered something under her breath to her partner. He stopped in his tracks and sauntered back towards me with a smug grin on his face. "Are you the guy who writes the ghost stories?" he asked. I said I was. "You don't half tell some far-fetched stories; where do you get them all from?" he asked, confrontationally.

"The public usually, or from research in libraries and such," I replied calmly, not taking the bait.

"That story about Jumping Jack leaping over rooftops, for example. That's a bit far-fetched, don't you think?" said the man, warming to his theme.

"Oh, you mean Spring-Heeled Jack?" I said, "Well, he was documented in hundreds of newspaper articles and seen by all sorts of witnesses over seven decades. Soldiers - including the Duke of Wellington, who hunted him, lawyers, doctors, policemen ... all reliable witnesses ... they all saw him. They saw something."

"You can't defeat gravity like that, jumping into the air that far. It's mad," said the man, with a hollow laugh.

"Do you believe it's possible for someone to walk across the sea? Or be in two places at once?" I asked the dog-walking sceptic. He shook his head with a smirk. "And just look at that," I said, nodding towards the three hundred and thirty-one-foot tall tower of the Anglican Cathedral, its top half missing because of the fog. "That cathedral was built on the strength of such tales. Christ walked on water, and after he rose from the dead, he was seen by two disciples walking to Emmaus, before vanishing and reappearing to the eleven apostles seconds later, and they were terrified because they thought he was a ghost."

"Well I'm an atheist; I don't believe all that stuff," said the cynic.

"Well, I do," put in his partner. "I'm a Christian, but I don't believe in ghosts."

I told her that ghosts were mentioned many times in the Bible, in the Book of Job, for example. I told her about the Witch of Endor summoning up the ghost of the dead prophet Samuel, and I told her what Jesus said to the disciples after he had risen from the dead. They thought the resurrected Christ was a spirit, but he allayed their fears by stating: "Look at my hands and my feet. It is I myself! Touch me and see; a ghost does not have flesh and bones, as you see I have." (Luke 24:39).

And then there was that line in the Bible, saying, 'And the disciples having seen him walking upon the sea, were troubled saying, "It is an apparition." and from the fear they cried out.'

At this point, the Atheist and the Christian rudely walked away, without any acknowledgement, and I had not even had a chance to mention Jesus talking with the ghosts of Moses and Elijah on the mountain, or the Biblical author of the Book of Hebrews, who says in (12:1) that spirits are all around us all the time. To me, the couple retreating into the fog symbolised the mindset of some people who have closed minds. Such people are often inconsistent too, avidly reading their newspaper horoscopes and picking their lucky Lotto numbers, yet pouring scorn on the idea of anything paranormal. Those people would certainly not give the following story any credence. It is the result of much research and numerous interviews with the descendants of the people mentioned in the tale, and hints at the possibility of beings who may live 'next door' to us in another dimension.

Mr Patrick Mooney, of Aspinall Street, Kirkdale, was highly disturbed by a mystifying thief. From the beginning of February 1895 he had noticed that various things: ornaments, books, keys, tobacco - even a string of sausages - had gone missing without a trace at his home. His wife worked, his children were at school, and Mr Mooney was employed at a relative's shop in West Derby, but whenever he or his wife returned home from work at around 5pm, they would find that something had been pilfered by the baffling bandit in their absence. The children were definitely not the culprits, because the thievery only happened when they were at school, and nothing ever went amiss on Saturdays or Sundays when they were all at home.

Mrs Mooney had her own theory; she believed that a woman named Mrs Hughes, who had once lived in their house as a lodger, had made a copy of their front door key, and was probably gaining access to the house in the afternoons, but it was later discovered that this Mrs Hughes had moved to Wolverhampton twelve months back to live with her sister, ruling that theory out.

Patrick Mooney was returning from work one day, and as he passed the police station on West Derby's Meadow Lane, he decided to go in and discuss the inexplicable disappearances of his property. Sergeant McIntosh, a square-shouldered, stern-looking individual, stood behind the counter, eyeing Mooney as he entered the station.

"I've come to ask for some advice, Sergeant," Mooney said meekly, looking at the three white chevrons on the policeman's arms.

"Advice about what, sir?"

"Well ... this may sound trivial ... but it's a matter of theft," Mooney told him.

"Theft is never a trivial matter, sir," was the

sergeant's grave response.

Mooney told the policeman all about the things that had gone missing from his home while he was away, and how it was bothering the whole family.

"Exactly when do you go out?" McIntosh asked, gazing through Mooney with a fixed steely blue-eyed gaze.

"Every weekday, from half-past eight in the morning till half-past-five in the afternoon."

"What about your wife and children?" asked Sergeant McIntosh. Mooney explained how his wife worked at a chandler's shop on Scotland Road each day and his children, of course, were at school.

"Then take a day off, hide somewhere in your home, and you may just find out who it is, sir," was the policeman's common sense suggestion, and Mooney decided that it was worth giving it a try.

Mooney's cousin, and employer, David, would only allow him to have the afternoon off, but a plan was put into operation. Mooney decided on the best place to stake out the living-room and kitchen - he crawled under the dining table and made himself comfortable, on a cushion with a flask of whisky at hand to keep him warm, and a carving knife to tackle the enigmatic pilferer, should he become dangerously violent.

At 2.15pm, he heard something rattling on the sideboard. Mooney peeped out from under the tablecloth and saw that it was Flynn, the family's young cat, pawing at a reel of thread. "Shoo!" hissed Mooney, startling the moggy, and it jumped off the sideboard and ran over to its wicker basket under a chair. After that false alarm, Mr Mooney settled back beneath the table, wondering if he would catch the culprit red-handed.

At 2.45pm Mooney heard a patter, and watched as Flynn's alert eyes looked over the basket rim at something in the corner of the room. The cat shrieked and ran off, and Mooney grasped the knife handle. He peeped out from under the fall of the tablecloth, and what he saw almost stopped his heart. A weird-looking dwarf, measuring no more than two feet in height, was standing on the corner of the hearth rug. He had a bald, grey, bullet-shaped head, little pointed ears, a pair of faintly lit menacing eyes, and a grinning mouth bursting with long discoloured fangs. He wore a single knee-length pleated strip of what looked like tabby-cat fur that was fashioned like a kilt. In one hand he carried a black sack, and the other hand rested on the handle of a small narrow-sheathed sword that was attached to his waist-belt.

Mooney scarcely dared breathe, his mind unable to take in the reality of the uncanny and surreal little man who was now tip-toeing past the table, brushing the tablecloth. A not unpleasant aroma, like cinnamon, greeted Mooney's nose as the unearthly creature passed by. Mooney tightened his grip on the handle of the carving knife with a shaking hand, as the little kilted figure suddenly scuttled silently in its bare feet towards the doorway, emitting a laryngitic wheeze as he did so. Then it vanished into the hallway.

With sweat beading on his forehead, Mooney quickly emerged from under the table, his heart pounding with fear of the unknown. Where on earth had this thing come from? and, more importantly, what the hell was it? He recalled the little sword which the diminutive little devil carried, and for one indecisive moment,

Mooney toyed with the idea of opening the window and climbing out to escape from the eerie intruder. Still unsure of the best course of action, he stepped backwards - on to the paw of his terrified cat Flynn, which reacted by screeching loudly and running off to hide.

The little grey man, startled by the cat's cry, let out a gruff grunt of surprise in the hallway. Mooney was standing rooted to the carpet, when suddenly, a fraction of the creepy little thief's head peeped out from the side of the door frame. A tiny pink eye with a burning pupil fixed Mooney in its sights, then, like lightning, the doll-sized oddity suddenly whizzed across the living-room from the hallway and darted into the wall to the right of the fireplace, as if there were a hole there - which, of course, there was not.

Even though the dwarf had now gone. Mooney was overwhelmed by the sensation of being watched, and he backed away into the hallway, with Flynn the cat following close on his heels. He opened the front door and staggered outside in a daze. The dull grey light of the overcast afternoon did not serve to allay Mooney"s fears of the little troll, and he quickly made his way to the chandler's shop on Scotland Road, to tell his wife all about the frightening occurrence.

Mrs Mooney knew at once that her husband had encountered something truly disturbing, just from the look of fear and confusion in his eyes, and she calmly told him to go and pick the children up from school and take them to her mother's home on Breeze Hill. Patrick Mooney willingly complied, only too glad to have something to do to take his mind off the afternoon's weird events, and also to postpone the time when he would be forced to go back into the house.

Later that evening, when the family had decided to stay at Mrs Mooney's mother's, at least for that night, and the children were tucked up in bed, Patrick Mooney went in search of an old friend who was very knowledgeable about all things supernatural. After many enquiries made in the pubs of north Liverpool, Mooney located this friend - Angus Kennedy - at Todd's Lodging House, in Islington's Clare Street. Angus was a man with an encyclopaedic knowledge of the unusual and the paranormal and had been, by trade, a professional clock and watch repairer until the demon drink had brought his career to an abrupt end. Mooney unburdened himself to Angus, telling him all about the strange little grey-skinned man and the items that had been regularly vanishing from his home. A dark cloud seemed to pass over Kennedy's face and, frowning, he thrust a brass poker into the glowing orange coals of the fire in the lodging house kitchen. After a few moments, he turned to face Patrick and said solemnly, "You have Takers in your home, Patrick, and I'm afraid the type you have described is particularly deadly."

"Takers?" repeated Mooney, intrigued by the unfamiliar term. "What exactly are they?"

"Well, it's my name for them," Kennedy told him with a wry smile, "but an accurate name, nevertheless. Thousands of objects ... and even people ... go missing without a trace every year. When you put your house keys down on a table and then suddenly discover they're not there, you put it down to your own absent mindedness, but what if that isn't the case at all?"

Kennedy took a small silver flask of whisky from the inside breast pocket of his coat, unscrewed the top, and closed his eyes to the incandescent coals, as he greedily drank the liquid fire.

"But what are they? and where are they from?" asked Mooney, as he found himself drawn to the lucent orange-hot landslide of coal and snow-white ash in the grate. Each little crevice looked more and more like a glowing cave in Hell.

"I haven't got a clue," admitted Kennedy, "but I believe in worlds within worlds. We are never alone in this universe; just think of the teeming life that shares this house ... everything from pinhole-boring bugs to rats ... I've counted over one hundred species of insects, mollusca and mammals that live in this lodging house, excluding the lodgers themselves ..." Here, Kennedy stopped for a moment and chuckled to himself, before resuming. "... Silverfish beetles, cheese mites, bats in the attic, centipedes ... the list goes on and on. Most of the time we're completely unaware of these life forms, and I believe there are also, right under our ignorant noses, other undiscovered realms. The Takers probably live in one of them. I've studied reports of these things for years. It usually starts with nothing more serious than a few missing items, but it can escalate very quickly and can end up in an insoluble murder, because sometimes when they're found out, the Takers choose to kill ..."

"We'll have to move house," Moooey interrupted, remembering all too vividly the fangs of that spine-chilling little figure. "There's nothing else for it."

"Yes, that would be a wise thing to do," his friend replied, without a moment's hesitation. "And I shall help you move, if you like."

That very night, Mrs Mooney - a highly superstitious woman - having heard his friend's theory about the Takers, held hands with her husband at her mother's house on Breeze Hill. She instructed him to fetch her dresses, underwear and all of the children's clothes from the house, and, of course, she also asked him to bring the cat Flynn as well. Mooney and Kennedy duly set off for the house in Aspinall Street at 8pm, and came upon a very sorry sight. The living-room had been totally ransacked. There was blood and scarlet paw-prints all over the tablecloth. Upstairs, Mr Mooney discovered that his daughter's antique rocking horse, which had been in the family for generations, was missing. This, more than anything else, enraged him, and he decided there and then to fight back.

"Flynn!"

Mooney nervously called for his cat with a lump in his throat, and Kennedy eventually found the animal, wounded, but alive and shaking, under an overturned bookcase in the living-room. The cat had sustained a minor injury to its front left paw, apparently inflicted by something sharp like a razor blade ... or a small sword! As Mooney tried to calm the terrified cat, he told Kennedy to get rid of the Takers. "Why should we move?" he ranted. "This is our house. Nobody has the right to take it off us."

Kennedy righted a chair then looked him directly in the eye, "Patrick, it would be much easier for you and your family if you did move."

But Mooney was having none of it, and he fetched an old hatchet from the coal cellar and began to examine the section of wall next to the fireplace.

"It disappeared into this exact spot," he told Kennedy. "You can't see where, but I saw it with my own eyes."

"Are you absolutely certain?" his friend asked, and Mooney nodded.

This piece of information seemed to change matters and Kennedy took a stub of chalk from his trouser pocket and sketched a strange seven-sided geometrical shape on to the wall where the Taker had disappeared. He then stood back, his eyes glued to the spot. Mooney swore with surprise as the chalked lines began to glow and shimmer with a dim crimson light.

"God help us!" muttered Kennedy, instinctively reaching for the whisky flask from the breast pocket of his coat. He unscrewed its cap with a trembling hand and emptied most of the contents into his mouth, as he gazed intently down the kaleidoscopic tunnel of rainbow light that had been opened up by the chalked heptagram. Mooney was completely dumbfounded. It all seemed so dreamlike; a tunnel, approximately three feet in diameter, running upwards at a slight incline for about thirty feet, and dappled with a spectrum of colours.

Three years ago, Kennedy had excitedly told Patrick Mooney that he had made a breakthrough in his occult practices, but had then collapsed from nervous exhaustion shortly afterwards. He had come close to being committed to an mental hospital, saved only by the intervention of his friend, who had looked after him for a while. On some nights, during that terrible period. Mooney had been forced to tie his friend to the bed up in the attic and gag him. Strange shadows darted about that attic when the 'mania' was upon him, and unearthly sounds were heard outside the window.

On one occasion, Mooney thought he saw a hole open up in the attic wall beside Kennedy's bed: it had been there one moment and gone the next. Kennedy had laughed hysterically when the inexplicable transient aperture appeared then vanished. That hole had kicked exactly like the one that Kennedy had just opened up in his own living-room, using his dark arts.

For several minutes, neither man was brave enough to venture into the cylindrical space. Then Patrick Mooney suddenly took a deep breath and crawled inside the tunnel carrying the coal hatchet. The tunnel walls felt smooth, glassy and cold to the touch. Kennedy followed him, shaking uncontrollably; his teeth were chattering not from fear, but from the accursed DT's. The two explorers soon reached a low-ceilinged cave bathed in a dim ruby-red light. There was sand, or possibly thick layers of dust - it was impossible to tell in the gloomy light - covering the floor, and it was peppered with little footprints of the Takers and two deep grooves leading to another tunnel that curved away into the unknown.

The place was filled with the rich aroma of cinnamon, strongly reminiscent of the odour of the Taker that Mooney had encountered in his home. Angus Kennedy drew his friend's attention to the mound of objects that lay partly buried in the dust on the floor. Mooney squatted down and began a hasty excavation with his hand and the hatchet blade: a ship in a bottle, blue-glass marbles, a pristine loaded flintlock pistol, a leather-cased captain's telescope, a Holy Chalice from some Christian church, and an all too familiar doll. It was Trudy, the beloved porcelain doll that Mooney's six-year-old daughter had 'lost' many months back. There were deep inhuman-looking teeth marks all over the doll's forehead and her dress was badly torn.

Kennedy brushed away the rusty powder on the floor to unearth what seemed to be a little wooden house. It made a whirring sound as the alcoholic mystic attempted to uproot it, and it soon revealed itself to be a cuckoo clock, as two doors in its facade swung open. The mechanical bird greeted him thrice: "Cuckoo! Cuckoo! Cuckoo!" Its little flue pipes sent the two-note calls echoing down the tunnels. Kennedy quickly dropped the clock, causing pink dust clouds to billow up from the impact. Mooney froze like a statue, with his eyes fixed on the end of the tunnel ahead. Nothing appeared.

"I don't like this. We should go back." was Kennedy's urgent suggestion, but Mooney cautiously made his way a little further down the tunnel, and soon noticed a side passage leading to a small cave where a dwarf-like creature sat, playing with a frog. The thing looked almost identical to the Taker he had encountered, only this one was really tiny - no more than ten inches tall - and from its wide eyes and innocent expression, it was obviously a 'child'. As the giant Mooney gazed down at it, the thing began to howl, revealing a set of tiny, but already nasty-looking fangs.

"Dar-dar!" it sobbed, and tears rolled down its grey plump cheeks. The unearthly child's cries quickly alerted what could only be its mother and father. They ran into the tunnel, full of concern. There he was. in the flesh, the Taker who had been ransacking

Mooney's house: the one who had injured the family's cat. The Taker stood protectively in front of a smaller, female version of himself, and drew his sword. It came screaming towards Mooney, skilfully twirling the blade of his weapon, obviously moving in for the kill.

Mooney's reactions were sluggish compared to the Taker's. He tried to parry the agile being's small but lethal sword with the head of the hatchet, but the blade sliced through his trousers at the right pocket. Luckily for Mooney, it cut through his leather tobacco pouch in the pocket, and so only grazed his skin. All the same, the Taker was now determined to pierce Mooocy's heart, and kept making sword-thrusts aimed at his chest. Mooney swung the hatchet wildly, determined to decapitate the miniature figure, but the Taker only emitted a sound like a choked chuckle, and retreated a short distance down the tunnel at lightning speed. Mooney suddenly recalled what Kennedy had told him about the thieving activities of the Takers sometimes ending in an insoluble murder. The Taker suddenly rushed forward again, gritting its fanged teeth, its eyes ablaze with anger, intending to skewer Mooney's heart, when there came a flash and a deafening bang. Angus Kennedy stood behind Mooney with a smoking flintlock in his shaking hand; it was the old gun he had retrieved from the dust with the other purloined items. By some miracle it had worked first time, and the lead ball had whizzed within an inch of Mooney's head.

The Taker was evidently terrified by the archaic weapon and after falling face down, he scrambled through the red dust over to his partner and child, and embraced them both. The Taker child by this time was hysterical.

"Let's be off now, Patrick," Kennedy advised his friend, and steered him back towards the tunnel. Mooney reluctantly allowed himself to be led away, but not before stooping down, and picking up a few of the items the Takers had robbed over the years, including the golden Holy Chalice, the ship in a bottle, and Trudy, the precious doll his daughter had been pining for since its disappearance.

"Patrick! What are you playing at?" an impatient Kennedy snapped, "This is not a game, you know. You've seen what these things can do. Let's be off ... now!" The two men quickly retraced their steps to the tunnel that led to the house on Aspinall Street and scrambled back down it. Mooney looked back just once, to see the Taker trying to pick up something he had stupidly left behind in his haste to get away - the hatchet! He tumbled out of the passageway into his living-room as the Taker, who was now in hot pursuit, abandoned the cumbersome hatchet and drew his sword instead.

Angus Kennedy quickly chalked a circle around the aperture on the wall, and hastily began to recite words Mooney had never heard before. Nothing happened. Kennedy swore and a nervous tic began to play on his face. The Taker, meanwhile, was charging down the passage, poised to strike with his lethal little sword. Kennedy spouted more esoteric phrases, and suddenly a deep groaning sound heralded the closure of the entrance to the Takers' world.

Mooney looked on dumbfounded as Kennedy sketched a symbol similar to a St Andrew's cross on the wall, and said that as long as that glyph stayed there, the Takers would be unable to gain entry back into the house. Kennedy made the occult sign permanent by touching it up with paint, and Mooney then wallpapered over it. However, one dark morning, a week later, the antique rocking horse the Taker had stolen from Patrick Mooney's daughter was found in the hallway - rocking gently back and forth - with Mooney's hatchet embedded in its head ...

Thankfully, the Takers never did return to the Mooney's house after that time, but whenever Mr and Mrs Mooney genuinely mislaid a pair of spectacles, or if Flynn the cat stole a sausage from the pantry, they would always find themselves imagining the worst for a while...

THE PELLEW STREET HORROR

Printed in Poland
by Amazon Fulfillment
Poland Sp. z o.o., Wrocław